Biblical Poems Embedded in Biblical Narratives

Biblical Poems Embedded in Biblical Narratives

Sharon R. Chace

WIPF & STOCK · Eugene, Oregon

BIBLICAL POEMS EMBEDDED IN BIBLICAL NARRATIVES

Copyright © 2020 Sharon R. Chace. All rights reserved. Except for brief quotations in critical publications or reviews, no part of this book may be reproduced in any manner without prior written permission from the publisher. Write: Permissions, Wipf and Stock Publishers, 199 W. 8th Ave., Suite 3, Eugene, OR 97401.

Wipf & Stock
An Imprint of Wipf and Stock Publishers
199 W. 8th Ave., Suite 3
Eugene, OR 97401

www.wipfandstock.com

PAPERBACK ISBN: 978-1-7252-6229-4
HARDCOVER ISBN: 978-1-7252-6230-0
EBOOK ISBN: 978-1-7252-6231-7

Manufactured in the U.S.A.   07/22/21

Dedicated to all the people on the front lines
fighting the pandemic of 2020

Connection of Presence

An ancient benediction
blooms anew as greeting.

Original context of suspicion
flowers as peace–filled trust.

Greetings! "While we are
absent one from another."

Not alone in knowing
nature can be cruel.

Not alone in this pandemic
practicing safety distance.

Not alone in shared hope
for saving sustenance.

Not alone in belief that
transcendent good will is.

Not alone.

This poem is based on an embedded covenant—verse or
benediction—poem in the Hebrew Bible or Old Testament. Forms
are fluid and multifaceted. The narrative context is the story of
Laban and Jacob making a covenant because they were not sure
if they trusted each other (Gen 31:43–55). Sometimes verse 49 is
used as a benediction in churches.

Therefore he called it Galeed, and the pillar Mizpah, for he said,
"The Lord watch between you and me, when we are absent
one from the other."

—GEN 31:48–49, NRSV

Contents

Acknowledgements

THANK YOU TO KAREN Barr Grossman for helping me with the author's guidelines and *The Chicago Manual of Style*. I deeply appreciate our friendship, conversations, and tea parties. Thank you to the editors of Wipf and Stock. My husband Ernest, "Ernie," gives time, thought, and driving skills that make my writing work easier. My daughter Amy is cheerleader and friend of all my books. The Rev. Derek van Gulden, pastor of the First Congregational Church of Rockport, Massachusetts offers encouraging words that help me to keep going.

Dear Pastors, Educators, and Readers

I AM AN OLDER, yet intellectually lively woman at this time serving a community as poet laureate of Rockport, Massachusetts. A member of the First Congregational Church of Rockport, I write as a liberal Christian and as a Jesuit-trained Protestant wildcard. My Master of Theological Studies degree with a biblical concentration is from Weston Jesuit School of Theology, 1998. I have one foot in the church and a big toe in academia. My books are in a wide variety of college and graduate-school libraries, including the libraries of Harvard Divinity School, Boston College School of Theology and Ministry, Azusa Pacific University, and my alma mater Albion College

Thank you for your interest in my exploration of biblical poems embedded in biblical narratives. My methodology is to: 1. Explore biblical poems that are embedded in biblical narratives; 2. Focus primarily on biblical poems that reflect some connection to forms of expression we use today including hymns, preaching, and benedictions. Following the introduction, each chapter contains two parts: my reflections and my suggestions to evoke response. Housekeeping notes: I have often aligned poetry to the left because poetry often changes when aligned in the middle. Therefore, if you own the book you have space for notetaking. Some sessions are longer than others; however, there is no need to complete all elements within one session. When classes are shorter, there is time to ask participants for feedback on which material has been most helpful.

While I intend this book primarily for people who lead a course or workshop, it may find a second audience in the workshop participants themselves. I am reminded of comments by a preschool teacher in Walpole, New Hampshire, around 1970 when my husband was pastor of the First Congregational Church. She said that her classes were based on the Sesame Street program the night before. "Everyone knew what we would be doing," she said. In addition to the teacher's cheerfulness, foreknowledge created security and happiness. Likewise, if class participants read ahead, they will know what to expect. For example, if someone reads my introduction before the first class session, he or she will become familiar with the concept of biblical poems inside prose and build a deeper understanding during their presentation.

Most leaders will be Christians but I hope that in many respects this book is bridge-building to people of other faiths and humanistic traditions. Some leaders will want to lead lectio divina. Other will not. I have experienced being lead in lectio divina and found that while I could not explain how it worked, it did. However, being a writer who reflects with pen in hand I am not likely to choose to lead this practice. Reflections through journal writing and lectio divina engage both hearts and minds. The first question at the end of each session is essentially what the leader would ask if leading lectio divina. Therefore lectio divina could be followed by considering the remaining questions and writing reflectively.[1]

Participants should bring a Bible, notebook, and pen or pencil. To my mind the best choices are the New Revised Standard Version or the Revised Standard Version. I discourage relying on The Message because it obliterates parallelism and rhythm which are key features of biblical poetry. If you wish, compare Philippians 2:1–11 in The Message and the Revised Standard Version. In the process of writing the first draft of this note, I discovered that the Common English Bible has a lectio divina version that could supplement my questions that prompt thought and journal reflections. This practice evokes imagination and supports a statement from biblical and

---

1. See Harrington, "Lectio Divina."

literary scholar, Amos N. Wilder. "It is at the level of the imagination that any full engagement with life takes place."[2]

Because of the honor of being Rockport's poet laureate I offer a poetry discussion group at a local nursing home so that older people can share their thoughts about poems and life. When I read *Wild Geese* by Mary Oliver, people automatically responded to their favorite phrase, as if they were practicing lectio divina. While not exactly sure what that means, I sense that lectio divina reflects a common thought process.

Rounding out my life by serving people with poetry is a privilege. This book is a late-in-life synthesis of my interests in art, biblical studies, and poetry. My hope is that my reflections will be an enjoyable way for people to learn about the literary artistry of biblical writers.

Grace and Peace,
Sharon
Winter, 2020

---

2. Wilder, *Theopoetic: Theology and the Religious Imagination*, 2.

Introduction

THE PURPOSE OF THIS course is to study biblical poems by focusing on those embedded in biblical narratives. Contemplating biblical poetry engages the imagination. Therefore literary reflection gives the reader a fuller appreciation than does the study of historical criticism alone, necessary as it is. The biblical scholar G. B. Caird wrote: "The creative act of imagination in which a poet gives birth to a metaphor, and the appreciative act of the reader who lays himself open to the resultant poem, allowing it to make its own impact on his mind, are both distinct from the act of the scholar who subjects the poem to critical study."[1] It seems to me that the thoughts of Caird and C. S. Lewis, Christian apologist and writer, intersect. In Lewis's chapter, "Bluspels and Flalansferes: A Semantic Nightmare" in *Selected Essays*, Lewis said that for him reason is the natural organ of truth, but imagination is the organ of meaning.[2] In an article titled "Can We Still Believe in Miracles? We Can, We Must" in *Commonweal*, Luke Timothy Johnson discusses the need for finding knowledge in fields other than empirical sciences. In his view, acknowledging religious experience and the truth-telling of myths (or stories, alternative word is mine) can help us imagine the world that Scripture imagines.[3] He goes on to say that myth is the proper

---

1. Caird, *Language and Imagery of the Bible*, 184.
2. Hooper, *Selected Literary Essays*, 265.
3. Johnson, "Can We Still Believe in Miracles?," 4–8.

language of the miraculous.[4] Consider the church historian Roland Bainton and his assessment of Martin Luther. Bainton said that Martin Luther verged on saying that an excessive emotional sensitivity is a mode of revelation.[5] Therefore imagination that is not part of strictly academic study can inform understandings of religious phenomena and poetry.

To my mind the prophets had a heightened sense of inspiration in which they imaginatively discerned the commands of God. Consider the poetic theory of Gerard Manley Hopkins in his letter about poetry to his friend, Alexander Baillie.

> I think then the language of verse may be divided into three kinds. The first and highest is poetry proper, the language of inspiration. The word inspiration need cause no difficulty. I mean by it a mood of great, abnormal in fact, mental acuteness, either energetic or receptive, according as the thoughts which arise in it seem generated by a stress and action of the brain, or to strike into it unasked. This mood arises from various causes, physical generally, as good health or state of the air or, prosaic as it is, length of time after a meal. But I need not go into this; all that it is needful to mark is, that the poetry of inspiration can only be written in this mood of mind, even if it only last a minute, by poets themselves.[6]

As an artist as well as poet, I partly understand. I did my best charcoal drawing as part of the final exam in a college studio art course. I was in a heightened sense of nervousness yet with more hand-eye coordination than usual. My strong, confident drawing strokes came from somewhere beyond my typical self. Energy and skill transcended my usual strength and ability. Was this inspiration from God or from the inner workings of my mind? Or does God work through human minds? I do not know. Whatever the source it was transcendent beyond everyday expertise.

---

4. Johnson, "Can We Still Believe in Miracles?," 7–8.

5. Bainton, *Here I Stand*, 283.

6. Pick, *Hopkins Reader*, 129.

Hopkins also weighed in on the place of imagination. In his essay "Poetic Diction" that he wrote for the Master of Balliol possibly in 1864, Hopkins notes the importance of diction as a defining characteristic of poetry. He refers to a variety of parallelism including that of the Hebrew Bible so he must have known of Lowth's work, which is discussed in more detail later in this introduction. He notes parallelism of both like and unlike lines. His conclusion is that imagination is part of both or, as he put it, looms over both.[7]

Does Hopkin's understanding neatly equate inspiration and imagination with truth? I do not think so. However his regard for inspired verse and imagination is significant. Furthermore Hopkin's readers have found insight and truths in his poetry.

If you question the validity of the imagination in discerning truth you are thoughtful and not alone. A basic question, as Alan Cooper put it in his chapter "Imagining Prophecy" in the book *Poetry and Prophecy: The Beginnings of a Literary Tradition*, edited by James L. Kugel, is whether the imagination can be a source of truth. He says that the pendulum swings back and forth. In a nutshell of his thought do imaginative writers play loose with facts or do they transcend facts for a nobler purpose?[8] I add that Picasso allegedly said that art can be a lie that tells you about the truth. Cooper goes on to say that poetry and prophecy raise essentially the same questions about the relationship between imagination and truth.[9] Walter Brueggemann also addresses the fictional nature in the biblical tradition of poetic utterance. In summary he says that the notion of fiction is not as easily dismissed as we might think because it is the work of fiction to probe beyond settled truth. In summary, settled truths such as customary understandings of biblical texts are shaped in our technological world that is bent towards problem solving but lacking in imagination, and mystery. The poet should not be dismissed as writing mere fiction. Brueggemann quotes the magisterial Roman Catholic scholar, Hans Urs von Balthasar,

7. Pick, *Hopkins Reader*, 136.
8. Cooper, "Imagining Prophecy," 42.
9. Cooper, "Imagining Prophecy," 42.

"God needs prophets to make himself known, and all prophets are necessarily artistic. What a prophet has to say can never be said in prose."[10]

The marker of validity of poetic and prophetic inspiration and imagination may be found in the words of Jesus in Matthew 12:33. A tree known by its fruits is like people known by their deeds and moral compass. Certainly the prophet Micah encourages the growth of healthy fruit of justice and kindness.

> He has told you, O mortal, what is good;
> and what does the LORD require of you
> but to do justice, and to love kindness,
> and to walk humbly with your God? (Mic 6:8)

I relate to imagining God's words. In approximately 1974 when my husband was pastor of the First Congregational Church of Walpole, New Hampshire, I wrote an imaginative dialogue essentially like the following.

God: Do you love your husband and child?

Sharon: Yes. You know that I do.

God: Do you write your poems?

Sharon: There isn't time. This parsonage is huge. There is so much cooking and cleaning. The phone rings and there are things to do with the Women's Fellowship.

God: You do not play your drum for me.

Sharon: I will.

If I literally heard those words it would have been time to call a mental health professional. Is there empirical evidence that I did imaginatively tap into what God called me to do? No, but there is a marker to measure validity. Is time for poetry writing what a wise person or loving parent would want for me? I believe that my dialogue led me to greater insight and, in time, the fruit of poetry.

I deeply appreciate the thoughts of John W. O'Malley, SJ, that he shared with me through correspondence. In summary, he loves the title of this course book because it gets at an aspect of the bible that at least hints at the ineffable that is God. When you

10. Brueggemann, *Finally Comes the Poet*, 4.

read biblical poetry, look for hints of the ineffable. Sharing a hint is a modest claim. You do not need to know for sure that you have unearthed a biblical author's experience of the ineffable. Too much certainty is the archenemy of wisdom.

While valuing imagination and experiences, I will not separate artistic, literary and religious experience from critical studies. The historical method is characterized by a high regard for human authors, their sources and life situations. Provenance of origin and authorship matters on the "Antiques Road Show" and in biblical studies. Context which is related to provenance also matters. Amy-Jill Levine says that there is an old saying in biblical studies that a text without context is just a pretext for making it say anything one wants. She credits Ben Witherington III for being the first to bring the saying to her attention. She goes on to say that knowing the original context leads to richer understanding.[11] The original context can inform the imagination and keeps interpretations from being too farfetched. Also critical studies help people avoid being trapped in intellectual prisons of biblical literalism. My blend of critical biblical studies, literary analysis, and personal applications is reflected in the division of each session into *reflection* and *response*.

You are probably wondering what I mean by poems embedded in narrative. The Psalms are poems that stand alone. Poems embedded in narrative are parts of biblical texts. For example, the well-known love chapter in 1 Corinthians 13 is to my mind a poem inserted into Paul's letter to a divided church I call "First Church Corinth." This chapter enumerates the attitudes that people in this early church or assembly needed in order to get along. Before we examine this poem and other embedded poems more fully, I will discuss the possibility of a continuum of poetry and prose in the Bible.

Is there a continuum of poetry and prose? In poetry writing groups I have attended there are ongoing discussions about what is and conversely what is not poetry. Thus it seems reasonable to me to expect a continuum in the Bible. However it is not clear that

---

11. Levine, *Short Stories by Jesus*, 9.

there is a continuum between poetry and prose in biblical literature. Scholars disagree. Therefore to some extent it depends upon
who you ask.

David L. Peterson says that Kugel argues that the distinction
between poetry and prose is best understood as involving different
points on a continuum. Thus there is no clear distinction.[12] In the
Art of Biblical Poetry, Alter says that it will not do to argue, as Kugel
does, that syntactic, rhythmic, and semantic strategies of biblical
verse are simply part of a continuum.[13] Peterson states that Alter
maintains that Hebrew prose is a natural expression of ancient Se-
mitic culture and Hebrew poetry is related to ethical monotheism,
unique to ancient Israel. To greatly simplify Peterson adds that
Alter finds parallelism and narrative in Hebrew poetry. So because
narrative is important in prose as well as poetry, Peterson thinks
Alter ultimately blurs the distinction.[14] Not sure about that! The
discussion goes on.

Amos N. Wilder, biblical scholar and poet, in his now classic book *The Language of the Gospel: Early Christian Rhetoric*, also
addresses the blurring of distinctions between biblical poetry and
prose. However the concept of continuum was not the way he
described distinctions between poetry and prose. He finds distinctive Hellenistic inspired, triple lines that balance. I have no idea
how he would respond to current studies in Johannine literature
that note ties with Palestine and thus make Hellenistic influences
less important. In any case balanced lines are poetic features. Nevertheless his finding of balanced lines is compelling. In his day the
Revised Standard Version (RSV) was the translation of scholarly
choice. So for that reason I quote his example of balanced lines
from the RSV that he altered slightly for unexplained reasons
but are likely his own translation of Koine Greek or his knowledge of ancient manuscripts. In my opinion the added words for
the purpose of inclusive language in the NRSV ruin the balance.
Wilder has definite ideas of what is and what is not poetry as we

12. Peterson and Richards, *Interpreting Hebrew Poetry*, 13.

13. Alter, *Art of Biblical Poetry*, 5.

14. Peterson and Richards, *Interpreting Hebrew Poetry*, 13.

will see in our study of 1 Corinthians. Meanwhile he mentions a middle ground. In referring to 1 John he says that this material is not poetry yet nevertheless is not prose. He finds passages in 1 John that are rooted or have background in Hellenistic thought and liturgy.[15] I add it is important to stress the rhythmic qualities throughout the Hebrew Bible or Old Testament and recent scholarship focusing on expanding the discussion of parallelism. Also themes of light and darkness are present throughout the Old and New Testaments.

> He who says he is in the light
> and hates his brother
> is in the darkness still.
> He who loves his brother
> abides in the light,
> and in it there are no pitfalls.
> But he who hates his brother
> as in the darkness
> and walks in the darkness.[16]

Perhaps the term "prose poem" is appropriate. In any case these verses are deeply embedded in narrative text because neither the RSV nor the NRSV set them apart or indent them as a poem. I appreciate reading these verses as a poem because the poetic arrangement adds focus and invites deeper consideration of meanings. Imagine the implications.

As noted in the introduction in *The Jewish Annotated New Testament*, unlike the Gospel of John, 1 John does not have a polemic attitude towards Jews.[17] Note that in that in 2:07 the author is not recording a new commandment. The love of brothers and sisters are rooted in the past and are flowing into the future. People of faith in God and/or humanity will find wisdom in 1 John.

15. Wilder, *Language of the Gospels*, 122–23.
16. 1 John 2:9–11, RSV and Wilder.
17. Murray, "First Letter of John," 448.

Bishop Robert Lowth

Bishop Robert Lowth was an eighteenth-century scholar who initiated the exploration of poetry in the Hebrew Bible or Old Testament. His work grew out of his examination of the poetry he found in the prophets. Large portions of prophetic books are poetry. When Jonah prays in the belly of the whale or great fish he prays in poetry (Jon 2:2–9). Consider a much loved poetic fragment in Mic 6:8. "He has told you, O mortal, what is good; and what does the Lord require of you but to do justice, and to love kindness, and to walk humbly with your God?" Notice the balance of lines and flow.

Lowth then discovered or discerned parallelism in other books of the Hebrew Bible. He gave biblical scholars "the eyes to see" in 1753 in his *Lectures on the Sacred Poetry of the Hebrews*. His work laid the foundation for mid-eighteenth-century German higher criticism.[18] This parallelism in his view has three types as pointed out by Adele Berlin in her essay "Introduction to Hebrew Poetry" in the *New Interpreter's Bible*.[19]

1. Synonymous. (The same basic idea in two lines)

2. Antithetic. (Opposing thoughts in two lines)

3. Synthetic. (Related lines that build or expand meanings)

An example of synonymous cited by Berlin is when two lines mean the same: "Praise the Lord, all you nations! // Extol him, all you peoples!" (Ps 117:1).

Lines that are basically the same can build in meanings not unlike synthetic lines. In his chapter "Ancient Hebrew Poetry," which is in the book *The Literary Guide to the Bible*, Robert Alter discusses parallelism that he calls "versets." This makes sense to me because "versets" implies poetic lines that are short poems. Even in lines that restate the basic idea, Alter finds movement and building-up of meanings. Such increase in meanings reminds me of Pantoum poems in which repeated lines expand meanings. Alter gives an example of repeated lines that add intensity. In his translation:

18. Richardson, *Emerson*, 12.

19. Keck et al., *New Interpreter's Bible*, 4:303–5.

I see the earth, and, look, chaos and void,
the heavens—their light is gone.
I see the mountains, and, look, they quake,
and all the hills shudder (Jer 4:23—24).

In my summary, the good creation as described in Genesis reverses back into chaos. In keeping with the consolation that Alter sees in Amos, Jeremiah, and Isaiah, and in order to clarify for myself and my readers, I add that eventually life will reverse back again as described in Jeremiah 31:2–3.

Thus says the Lord:
the people who survived the sword
found grace in the wilderness;
when Israel sought for rest,
the Lord appeared to him from far away.
I have loved you with an everlasting love;
therefore I have continued my faithfulness to you.

Alter sees biblical poetic images such as Isaiah 35:1, "The wilderness and the dry land shall be glad, the desert shall rejoice and blossom like the crocus (Ed note: or rose in popular usage); it shall blossom abundantly," as about more than return from exile. He emphasizes the blossoming and perfect peace (based on Isaiah 26:03). To paraphrase: The poetic medium, he says, reinforces the vision of future, apocalyptic renewal and redemption in a way the biblical prose writers had not done. I quote his very significant sentences. "The matrix, then, of both the apocalyptic imagination and the messianic vision of redemption may well be the distinctive structure of ancient Hebrew verse. This would be the most historically fateful illustration of a fundamental rule bearing on form and meaning in the Bible. We need to read the poetry well because it is not merely a means of heightening or dramatizing the religious perceptions of the biblical writers—it is the dynamic shaping instrument through which those perceptions discovered their immanent truth."[20]

---

20. Alter and Kermode, *Literary Guide,* 623.

Sometimes poets discover their truths through striving and structuring their poems to make their thoughts clear. Poetry structured with the purpose of conveying the promise of reversals conveys faith that in time fairness wins. Consider Mary's song of reversals that suggests healing for broken selves. What then, you might ask, is the distinctive structure of New Testament poetry? I do not know, yet I have thoughts. I doubt that there is one distinctive feature that applies to all New Testament poetry. However, there is a common marker which is the reversal of unjust situations and a fallen world. Ponder the reversals or compensations proclaimed in the poetic beatitudes which are as close as possible to Jesus' exact words. Believe in John of Patmos's conviction that God will wipe away tears in an eschatological event or a more immanent experience through the gifts of understanding people in the present.

My sense of a common marker seems not unlike sightings of a distinctive structure in which reversals matter. It seems to me that when biblical writers see the truth that redemption matters and write their visions in parallel lines, truth and beauty merge. Is there a specifically Christian characteristic? For some, the resurrection, however it is understood, can be considered the ultimate reversal.

I add a New Testament example of contrasting parallel lines because as an artist I find it visually compelling. I also value it as a summary of who Jesus was in his time and place.

Matthew wrote two opposing or antithetical parallel lines that summarize one understanding of Jesus' identity as a wandering scribe. After the "Sermon on the Mount" in Matthew 5–7, which is Matthew's compilation of the sayings and teachings of the Jesus, Matthew reports that Jesus instructed unnamed people to cross to the other side. A scribe told Jesus that he would follow him wherever he went. This was nervy because Jesus invited followers rather than asking for volunteers. The title "Son of Man" has different connotations throughout the New Testament. In this case it is Jesus' way of talking about himself. Jesus replied, "Foxes have holes, and birds of the air have nests; // but the Son of Man has nowhere to lay his head" (Matt 8:20). Unlike Jesus the scribe had a lifestyle that needed a stable home life. These parallel lines give a picture of animals and birds with snug homes that are in sharp contrast to the homelessness of Jesus, although he had hospitable friends including Mary and Martha. Matthew's first audience to whom he wrote his Gospel could readily imagine the foxes and birds. Likewise people today can picture foxes and birds. This visual image connects present-day readers with ancient literature. Is this image in parallel lines a poem? It has more syllables than a haiku but is not a short form that is recognized as a poem. There is room for ambiguity. In any case it has poetic compactness that summarizes the main point. Brevity zooms to essence. The essence here is a summary of Jesus' identity as a wandering sage which is one aspect of his earthly life. I consider these parallel lines to be a poem embedded in poetic prose.

Matthew's depiction of Jesus as a wandering sage underscores Jesus as a source of wisdom. Scribes in Jesus' day were literate and wise, so the inclusion of the scribe furthers the theme of wisdom in Matthew's writings. The "Sermon on the Mount" that precedes Jesus conversation with the scribe is a wisdom instruction foreshadowed by the visit of the wise men to Jesus on the first Noel. Jesus as a wise sage can be embraced by theists, humanists, and even atheists. Reflective people can probe the teachings of Jesus for insights about the human condition and meanings in life. Jesus as sage offers thoughts for both poets and biblical exegetes.

Synthetic parallelism is complicated enough that it has kept scholars busy since around 1980. It is a catchall term for lines that are not clearly the same or opposite. Often in synthetic lines one line clarifies or adds meaning. One example that is clear-cut: "Fools say in their hearts, 'There is no God'/ They are corrupt, / they do abominable deeds; // there is no one who does good" (Ps 14:1). These two lines are synthetic because the second line clarifies and adds meaning to the first line.

James L. Kugel has a take on parallelism that seems broader, although not more simple. He writes: "Poetry in many languages is written in some sort of identifiable meter. Rhyme also characterizes the poetry of many different people. The poetry of the Bible, by contrast, has neither rhyme nor fixed meter. Instead it is characterized by an ideal sentence form that is repeated line after line."[21] Similarly David L. Paterson writes, "In sum, Hebrew poetry possesses rhythm, not meter."[22]

Continuing the Discussion Beyond Bishop Robert Lowth's Findings

Parallelism is still very important and part of the ongoing discussion of biblical poetry. New studies that view parallelism through metrical, lexical, and grammatical analysis are important yet seem to me to be complicated expansions of Lowth's original findings. Because parallelism can also be a part of prose, it does not automatically mean poetry but it is a big hint that two or more parallel verses are at least poetic snippets if not full-bodied poems. You may wonder if parallelism is found mostly in the Old Testament or Hebrew Bible. Not exclusively—the New Testament contains parallel verses. Here are two sets:

Here is a synonymous verse of basically the same meanings. "For who has known the mind of the Lord? //Or who has been his / counselor?"(Rom 11:34). In my NRSV those words are indented to signify poetry. English translations of the Bible sometimes make it easy to discover biblical poems embedded in narrative because translators indent the words they deem to be poetry. Yet as we have seen in Matthew's Gospel, you may find biblical passages that are poems or poetic fragments which are not indented.

The following quotations are not indented and, therefore, are more deeply embedded in narratives. Contrasting or antithetic lines are: "For the wages of sin is death, //but the free gift of God is eternal life in Christ Jesus our lord" (Rom 6:23).

In synthetic parallelism that second line completes the first. "For now we see in a mirror, dimly, but then we will see face to

---

21. Kugel, *Great Poems of the Bible*, 19.

22. Peterson and Richards, *Interpreting Hebrew Poetry*, 47.

face./ Now I know only in part; then I will know fully, even as I have been fully known" (1 Cor 13:12).

In addition to parallelism, there are other characteristics of biblical poetry including consideration of line, rhythm, imagery, movement, terseness. Adele Berlin identified these markers.[23] But I also found these characteristics, especially movement, when I helped my seminarian husband with his exegetical homework in 1968. My findings are important to note because my English minor in college predisposed me to see these literary qualities. Therefore undergraduate study of English literature might help seminarians grapple with biblical studies. According to Robert Alter in his book *The Art of Biblical Poetry*, movement was close to the way that biblical poets expected audiences to attend to their words.[24] Movement as flow continues to be a feature of poetry.

The definition of poetry in *Literary Forms in the New Testament: A Handbook* by James L. Bailey and Lyle D. Vander Broek provides a working definition of poetry. "Although poetry has evolved over the years, it is quite possible to give a general definition of the forms that applies to both first-century and modern expressions. Firstly, poetry often contains figurative language. Instead of simply stating directly the thoughts she or he wishes to convey, the poet uses word pictures, images, symbols, metaphors and so forth, to encourage the reader to wrestle with the issues at hand."[25] Secondly there is rhythm. Rhythm may create a kind of meter as previously mentioned. However meter in a formal sense as in iambic pentameter is absent in biblical poems.

Let us consider three features of biblical poems that are embedded in narratives.

1. Metaphors and Similes.
2. Memory aide.
3. Summaries.
4. Assurances of divine love.

23. Berlin, "Introduction to Hebrew Poetry," 302–3.
24. Alter, *Art of Biblical Poetry*, 9.
25. Bailey and Vander Broek, *Literary Forms in the New Testament*, 76–77.

Metaphors and Similes

Metaphors and similes abound in the Bible. Similes use the word "like" and basically function as metaphors. In Matthew 13, there are poetic verses describing the kingdom as like, for example, a mustard seed or treasure in a field. As we have seen, there is scholarly debate as to whether or not there is a continuum of poetry and prose in the bible. I vote yes based on the kingdom similes that seem to be to be like Wilder's middle ground somewhere between poetry and prose. For now, let us consider two metaphors that are in embedded poems. Genesis 49 is mostly poetry. Jacob speaks in a long poem. In verse 24 there is a double metaphor for God. Rock and Shepherd: "Yet his bow remained taut, and his arms were made agile . . . by the name of the Shepherd, the Rock of Israel." In Deuteronomy 32, "Rock" is a repeated metaphor for God with the Hebrews having the true rock in contrast to the inferior god or rocks of their enemies. Rock as a metaphor is also used often in the Psalms that are stand-alone poems as a symbolic or metaphor for God. As a metaphor "rock" is a stock image or cliché. However, stock images can convey time-honored truths.

Job has a prose introduction and a prose ending. The middle is one long poem—basically chapter 3 through the first part of chapter 42. In chapter 3 of Job, Job curses the day he was born. His poem is filled with darkness and despair. Fast-forward to 38:8–11 where the primordial mists over the surface of the deep are called "swaddling bands," a metaphor that is unique in biblical literature according to Robert Alter.[26] Those bands curtail the powers of chaos and evil symbolized in the chaos of the seas and thus are protective. I add that Christians will associate those bands with the swaddling bands in which Mary wrapped the infant Jesus to keep him protected and warm. Thus the image of "swaddling bands" in the Old Testament enriches readers of the New Testament.

The writer of Job created a metaphor that rises above clichés and received truths. In the end, life and God work out well for Job. You may not agree. After all a new set of children are

---

26. Alter, *Art of Biblical Poetry*, 123–24.

not replacement parts for the lost children. One way to look at this problem is to think that the story of Job is open-ended. My personal way of dealing with the questions of theodicy that the ending poses is to return to Job 38–41. God's poem is filled with light and wisdom. Animals are part of creation. Some animals eat others. Death begets life. There is savage beauty in give and take. The horse and the Leviathan surge with power granted by God. In a birth image of new life God asks Job if he knows when the mountains give birth or in the next line, that adds intensity, when the deer calve (39:1). Two parallel lines reinforce the other. God revealed through the reader's inner wisdom and imagination gets right to a main concern.

> Who has put wisdom in the inward parts,
> or given understanding to the mind? (Job 38:36)

God's voice from the whirlwind evokes regard for God's power and for some readers trust. Considering is what poets and thoughtful preachers do. I ask and invite my readers' consideration of the question: Is God's poem truth or is it temporal ambiguity creating room for beauty's mystery?

Memory Aid

Memory is important in many religions yet is especially important in Judaism. No wonder that a Hebrew scholar, Harold Fisch, discusses the purpose of biblical poems in helping people to remember what is important. He states: "Moses is instructed to write a poem before he dies, a poem that will live unforgotten in the mouths and minds of the people.[27] In some translations the word "poem" is "song." I will use Fisch's translation. "Now therefore, write you this poem, and teach it to the children of Israel; put it in their mouths, that this poem may be a witness for me against the children of Israel" (Deut 31:19). In 32:4, which is Moses' song or poem, Moses proclaims the name of the Lord. "The Rock, his work is perfect, and all his ways are just. // A faithful God, without

27. Fisch, *Poetry with a Purpose*, 50–51.

deceit, just and upright is he." Then God explains that in the land of milk and honey the Israelites will turn to other gods and forget their God. So the poem or song that predicts this apostasy will be a witness. In the end though, God does vindicate his people, and the enemies with their lesser rock will be vanquished.

Over centuries the Shema found in Deuteronomy 6:4–9, which is a basic statement of faith, will have continuity through repetition and new applications. Consider the first two verses of the Shema: "Hear, O Israel: The Lord is our God, the Lord alone. You shall love the Lord your God with all your heart, and with all your soul, and with all your might" (Deut 6:4–5). The poetry of biblical times and of the present day can help people remember what is important. Luke 10:27 records Jesus' quotation of this passage to a lawyer who asked about eternal life. Because Luke uses Jesus' quotation of the Shema to introduce the parable of the Good Samaritan, Luke adds the word "neighbor."

Summaries

Sometimes biblical poems (or so it seems to me) serve as summaries. To my mind, summaries are important because they are usually short and engage imagination. As I have said before, brevity zooms to essence. The mission of John the Baptist, the characteristics of vibrant life in faith communities, and the essence of faith as assurance of God's love are summarized in embedded poems.

Summaries of the Mission of John the Baptist

Let us pause to compare summaries in our Bibles. All four Gospels summarize the mission of John the Baptist with the same basic idea in slightly different versions (Matt 3:3; Mark 1:2–3; Luke 7:27; John 1:23). In Matthew there is a prose introduction in the first part of 3:3: "This is the one of whom the prophet Isaiah spoke when he said . . ." The rest of verse 3 is poetry. In summary, John's mission is to prepare the way of the Lord.

Readers who have not studied the Bible critically might wonder why the verses are slightly different. So I want to explain the synoptic problem as simply as possible. Although you can study biblical poetry without referring to the synoptic problem, it is a foundational concept in critical biblical studies. The Synoptic Gospels are Matthew, Mark, and Luke. They are called synoptic because they tell the story of Jesus in about the same way. Basically the synoptic problem is figuring out why there are differences in the three gospels that are in sync. Mark was the first gospel to be written. Matthew and Luke used his basic outline and changed some wording. Matthew and Luke had sources that Mark did not have. The summary of John's ministry is one of the few times that the Synoptic Gospels and the Gospel of John have about the same account. Still when I asked the late Daniel J. Harrington, SJ, with whom I studied at Weston Jesuit School of Theology if there is any evidence that the author of John knew Mark's Gospel, he said, "Not much."

Simeon, the devout Hebrew priest who welcomed Jesus according to custom into community, summarizes the mission of Jesus to be "a light for revelation to the Gentiles" (Luke 2:29–32). By including Simeon's poem of praise Luke emphasized the inclusion of gentiles in the family of God. Luke and his Gospel foreshadow the gentile mission.

Poets speak to other poets and thus build bridges spanning centuries. While not gathered physically in the same room, converging ideas form imaginary conversations. Considering the thoughts of biblical poets can help readers of biblical literature understand the faith of the biblical poets and the piety of their original audience. Contemporary poets might find parallelism, diction or mood as features to consider. People of faith will experience richness in discovering the development of biblical thought.

Consider Isaiah, Luke, Simeon, and me as poetic associates. The prophet Isaiah is charged with making sure that Israel will be a light not only to the tribes of Israel but to the world. The context was still Judaism but also an opening and expanding stance.

> And now the LORD says,
> who formed me in the womb to be his servant,
> to bring Jacob back to him,
> and that Israel might be gathered to him,
> for I am honored in the sight of the LORD,
> and my God has become my strength—
> he says,
> It is too light a thing that you should be my servant
> to raise up the tribes of Jacob
> and to restore the survivors of Israel;
> I will give you as a light to the nations,
> that my salvation may reach to the end of the earth.
> (Isa 49:5–6)

Luke shaped poetic words from Simeon's faith that incorporated Isaiah's vision. In Luke's story (2:21–40), which reveals Jesus as a "light for revelation" to the gentiles and foreshadows his life, Simeon is a devout man looking forward to the consolation of Israel. He knew through the Holy Spirit that he would not die before he had seen the Lord's Christ. Taking Jesus in his arms, he praised God, saying:

> Master, now you are dismissing
> your servant in peace,
> according to your word;
> for my eyes have seen your
> salvation,
> which you have prepared in the
> presence of all peoples,
> a light for revelation to the Gentiles
> and for glory to your people Israel. (Luke 2:29–32)

Inspired by Isaiah, Luke, and Simeon, I wrote the following Pantoum poem.

> Presentment: Luke 2:33–35
> Good priest Simeon welcomes the infant Jesus
> circumcising him into community and continuity.
> Tells Mary and Joseph about life ahead on the way
> "He will be a light for revelation to the Gentiles."

Circumcising him into community and continuity,
"A sword will pierce your innermost being.
He will be a light for revelation to the Gentiles
and a glory for your people Israel."

"A sword will pierce your innermost being."
Tells Mary and Joseph about life ahead on the way
and a glory for your people Israel,
Good priest Simeon welcomes the infant Jesus.

Vibrant Life in Faith Communities

Embedded poems in 2 Chronicles and 1 Peter suggest characteristics that create vibrant faith communities. In 2 Chronicles 6:41–42, Solomon prays to God during the dedication of the temple. God is invited to rest with the ark in the temple.

> Now rise up, O Lord God, and go to your resting place,
>   you and the ark of your might.
>
> Let your priests, O Lord God, be clothed with salvation,
>   and let your faithful rejoice in your goodness.
>
> O Lord God, do not reject your anointed one.
>   Remember your steadfast love for your servant David.

After the dedication of the temple, faithful people in the Chronicler's account rejoice in God's glory and offer praise. This embedded song or poem or prayer proclaims trust: "For he is good,// for his steadfast love endures forever" (2 Chr 7:3). What a wonderful inter-faith affirmation for worshiping communities!

In 1 Peter turning away from evil and seeking peace are actions that keep many kinds of associations vital. Let us read 1 Peter 3:10–12.

These verses are a poem embedded in prose, which is a household code. Not only is this poem embedded in prose, it is also deeply enmeshed in the culture of earliest Christianity. The people of the faith community in 1 Peter felt like aliens and exiles in constant danger of being persecuted by the dominant culture. The strategy for survival was cultural conservatism. Honor the Emperor. "Participate in imperial rites but remember you belong to Christ" is a summary of the stance that was helpful at the time. The household code of chapter 3 is part of that approach. Suffering abuse and returning mistreatment with a blessing does not sanction domestic violence today. However, this poem transcends its cultural matrix. In my opinion this poem is more that summery. It is a thoughtful pondering about long-range implications. Rejoicing in God's steadfast love and seeking peace are interfaith practice. I wondered if this gifted poet would have the generous understanding of the community of Peter being part of the chosen, holy people instead of replacing their Jewish forefathers and foremothers. His poem is so broadly applicable that I believe the answer is "Yes."

First Peter is attributed to Peter but it is pseudonymous. A fisherman from Galilee would not have used the quality of Greek in this book. I am grateful to an unknown poet whose words hint at the ineffable.

> Those who desire life
> and desire to see good days,
> let them keep their tongues from evil
> and their lips from speaking deceit;
> let them turn away from evil and do good;
> let them seek peace and pursue it.
> For the eyes of the LORD are on the righteous,
> and his ears are open to their prayer.
> But the face of the LORD is against those who do evil.

Assurance of God's Love

Throughout the Old Testament God is praised for his covenantal, steadfast love.

The promise of enduring, steadfast love reminds me of Romans 8:31–39 which is poetic prose—especially verses 35–39. These verses were arranged as a poem based on the RSV in the

Introduction

PILGRIM HYMNAL, the hymnal of my youth. Daniel J. Harrington, SJ said without going into detail, almost as an aside, that arguably Romans 8 is the most important chapter in the New Testament.

> If God is for us, who is against us? He who did not spare his own Son but gave him up for us all, will he not also give us all things with him? . . .
> Who shall separate us from the love of Christ? Shall tribulation, or distress, or persecution, or famine, or nakedness, or peril, or sword? . . .
> No, in all these things we are more than conquerors through him who loved us. For I am sure that neither death, nor life, nor angels, nor principalities, nor things present, nor things to come, nor powers, nor height, nor depth, nor anything else in all creation, will be able to separate us from the love of God in Christ Jesus our LORD. (Rom 8:31–32, 35, 37–39, RSV)

When I was a senior in high school, several classmates lost a parent through death. I wrote out this arrangement from Romans 8 in each sympathy card. Another New Testament passage that is definitely an embedded poem dovetailing with covenantal steadfast love is Revelation 21:3–4. In Revelation the promise of God with us is in part eschatological or in the future. However the future does not have to mean the distant future. The future can be understood as in the present after a time of working through grief. Also, biblical passages often have counterbalancing thoughts. Matthew 28:20 clearly suggests God's immanent presence with the promise that God is with us, always. The promise that God is with us in the present (Matthew) and will wipe away every tear in the future whether near or distant (Revelation) is steadfast love. The overall interfaith thrust is that death does not have the last word.

Bibical Poems Inside Prose

Welcome and Introduction

1. Each person states his or her name and where he or she lives, followed by a few sentences about oneself.

2. The leader speaks about his or her background, education, and publishing history.

3. The leader reads the introduction or, more likely, reads highlights from it. Optionally, participants may take turns reading the introduction. I am not the only person who benefits from rereading. Therefore, even if people have read the introduction previously, rereading can be beneficial.

   Introducing the concept of biblical poems inside prose could be as basic as the following summary. Biblical poems that are embedded in narratives are poems that are inside, sometimes even hidden in prose. In contrast, the Psalms are poems that stand alone.

   The hallmark of biblical poetry is parallelism. Parallel lines can express the same essential idea, or contrasting ideas, or lines of thought that build in meaning. Today, we will focus on two lines that are contrasting or opposing. "Foxes have holes, and birds of the air have nests, but the Son of Man has nowhere to lay his head" (Matt 8:20). These lines that describe Jesus as a wandering sage can be appreciated by people of many religious and humanist persuasions. The leader might want to read my discussions about these two lines within the introduction.

4. Questions from the group and discussion.

Mary's Poem

Luke 1:46–55

Reflection: General Background

LET US START WITH the author of Luke, who I will call Luke in regard to tradition. He presents Mary's poem to his original audience. Therefore his summary of Mary's ponderings was not written to us but Mary's poem is for us. Who was Luke? Luke was an anonymous writer and editor, who specialized in salvation history. Because he was literary, thoughtful, and calm, he was well-suited to his self-assigned task of writing an orderly account of learned truths to his patron Theophilus. In Greek, Theophilus means "lover of God."

When did Luke write and when? Luke wrote his Gospel between 85 and 90 AD. He also wrote Acts. Therefore Luke and Acts are a two-volume set that give glimpses of Luke's themes. He most likely wrote to the churches that were influenced by Paul. Southern Greece may have been the place of composition.

Luke was concerned for the lost, poor, and lonely. It is very important to note that the Jewish system mandated concern for the poor, according to Amy-Jill Levine. Therefore, concern for the poor is rooted in Judaism, not a new development in the early church. Dr. Levine wrote the introduction to Luke in *The Jewish Annotated New Testament*. She said: "To regard Jesus, appropriately, as caring for women, children, the sick and the poor, embeds him within Judaism rather than separates him from it."

Luke wrote stories to express his concerns and trusts in God that there will be reversals. In chapter 15 there are three stories that show Jesus' concern for the lost. Luke selected these stories from his (metaphorically speaking) manuscript pile and grouped them together in a collection. Taken together they are like rich, painterly impasto, which means thick, highly textured paint. These stories are the parable of the lost sheep (vv. 1–7), the parable of the lost coin (vv. 8–10), and the parable of the prodigal son and his elder brother in the remaining verses. The story of the prodigal son is the most fully developed story and climax of this three-parable set. Clearly Luke had storytelling talents that are well-known. He used narrative to support his beliefs about the worth of all people, worthy of healing and salvation.

Yet Luke was also a poet. It takes a poet to name God, "The Author of Life" (Acts 3:15)! Poets also distill the most important meanings. As noted in the introduction, when righteous and devout Simeon took the infant Jesus into his arms, he praised God in poetry (2:29–32). Distilling the meaning of Jesus, Simeon says that Jesus is "a light for revelation to the Gentiles." To my mind this distillation is both literary foreshadowing and prophetic proclamation.

As a poet Luke seems to have had knowledge of long-standing literary traditions that some people of his day would have known. Luke gives us a glimpse of Paul preaching in poetry to the Athenians. You might say that both Luke and Paul recommend the poem of an ancient poet to Athenians. We will see more of Paul's poetic preaching in the next chapter. When Paul was in Athens he told the Athenians that he knew they were religious because he had found an altar to the "unknown god." Paul went on to say that the Athenians would perhaps grope for and find God, who is not far from us. For "'In him we live and move and have our being'; as even some of your own poets have said, 'For we too are his offspring'" (Acts 17:28). According to the study notes in the

Harper Collins Study Bible, the quotation that begins with "For, in him" may come from the sixth-century-BCE philosopher-poet, Epimenides. The phrase "For we too are his offspring" came from a third-century-BCE poet, Aratus. Luke uses the poetry his listeners would have known in order to convince them that his God is worthy of devotion. Therefore he was not afraid to use culture as a lens to view religious beliefs. The contemporary approach that is similar is to discuss religious issues or ethics that are addressed in contemporary film.

Another indicator that Paul knew ancient literature is found in the book of Acts. Paul was sent on a boat to Italy with other prisoners. A northeast storm blows up. An angel tells Paul that he must stand before the emperor so safety would be granted to all on board. Paul tells the men to keep up their courage for he has faith in God. Eating together in a way that echoes the Eucharist, the prisoners regain strength. After striking a reef, the prisoners were told to swim for shore. All were brought to safety. This story is in high contrast with the shipwreck in *The Odyssey*. Shipwrecked sailors in that story do not survive. Luke's readers would get the point that Luke's God is stronger than Zeus. Faithful fiction conveys truths. Brueggemann points out that Hans Urs von Balthasar, the Roman Catholic scholar, has said that God needs prophets, and all prophets are artistic. What a prophet has to say can never be said in prose.[1] Remember Lowth's initial study of the poetry of the Hebrew prophets. Brueggemann goes on to say that poetic-prophetic utterance runs the risk of being heard as falsehood.[2] However, in summary, he goes on to say that the notion of fiction is not as precarious as we might imagine. Fiction probes beyond settled truth and opens the way for transformation and the gift of newness.[3] Prophetic poems, the testimonies of early Christians, spoke about new possibilities in fiction more powerful than facts.[4] If my understanding and simplification of Brueggemann's favored word "entrenched" is correct, it

1. Brueggemann, *Finally Comes the Poet*, 4.
2. Brueggemann, *Finally Comes the Poet*, 5.
3. Brueggemann, *Finally Comes the Poet*, 5.
4. Brueggemann, *Finally Comes the Poet*, 6.

means today being stuck in a mechanistic worldview where prose is the only means of expressing truth. In this worldview, spiritual experience is reduced or limited to what can be explained through factual prose. So if the poetry of the prophets (including Jesus), the songwriters, and prayers strike you as fiction, ask what truth or fresh understandings these writings open up for you. Perhaps reading poetry, historical fiction, or practicing Lectio Divina and journal writing can help.

Luke 1:46–55: The Background of Mary's Song

Mary's poem or song is embedded in the narrative or story of Mary's visit to Elizabeth (Luke 1:39–56). I personally believe that this story reflects a very happy time for Mary and Elizabeth, both pregnant with a lot of personal and family matters to discuss. How wonderful to have this social time together before life starts to get harder for both Elizabeth and Mary. When Elizabeth hears Mary's greeting the child within her jumps for joy. Even before John is born he is already announcing both Luke's theme and the coming of Jesus who will be joy for the world. Joy is one of Luke's favorite themes.

Luke's composition is based on his understanding of Mary's heart, and echoes Hannah's song in 1 Samuel 2:1–10 about Jesus' birth. The first readers of Mary's poem or song might have said, "We have seen something like this before." God rescued Hannah from disgrace in her community when Hannah became pregnant and thus fulfilled her womanly role. This was a huge reversal from shame to acceptance and rejoicing. Hannah's song praises God for the salvation of the oppressed. Hannah was Mary's historical soul sister. Jocelyn McWhirter, professor and chair of the religious studies department at Albion College, says (in summary) that Mary, the mother of Jesus, reaffirms what Hannah, the mother of Samuel, has already proclaimed: that God exalts the poor, the hungry, the lowly."[5] In God's eyes, over time, and in the sightings of people who value the poor, Hannah and Mary are exalted.

---

5. McWhirter, *Rejected Prophets*, 41.

Hannah's song and Mary's song both have the poetic characteristic of parallelism. From Hannah's song: "He raises up the poor
from the dust; / he lifts the needy from the ash heap"(1 Sam 2:8).
From Mary's song: "He has brought down the powerful from their
thrones, and lifted up the lowly; he has filled the hungry with good
things, and sent the rich away empty" (Luke 1:52–53). These parallel verses of reversals and turn-around are poetry inserted into the
narrative. As we have seen, when poetry is inside another form of
biblical writing, the poetic lines summarize central ideas. Mary's
poem distills and foreshadows the essence of Jesus' ministry.

The Text: Response

Read Mary's song out loud together or ask someone in the class to
read it aloud. In addition to providing a summary of the importance of concern for the poor and the hope of reversals, consider
other poetic features. There is cadence in the parallelism. Two-line
verses repeating is an artistic way that reinforces the claims. The
word "for" is repeated as emphasis that God favors the poor. Verbs
are strong yet in the past tense, perhaps suggesting that the reversals have started, a kind of realized eschatology, in the present that
is initiated by the historical Jesus.

Mary's Song of Praise

And Mary said,
"My soul magnifies the LORD,
and my spirit rejoices in God my Savior,
for he has looked with favor on the lowliness of his servant.
Surely, from now on all generations will call me blessed;
for the Mighty One has done great things for me,
and holy is his name.
His mercy is for those who fear him
from generation to generation.
He has shown strength with his arm;
he has scattered the proud in the thoughts of their hearts.
He has brought down the powerful from their thrones,
and lifted up the lowly;

he has filled the hungry with good things,
and sent the rich away empty.
He has helped his servant Israel,
in remembrance of his mercy,
according to the promise he made to our ancestors,
to Abraham and to his descendants forever. (Luke 1:46–55)

The World in Front of the Text: Lectio Divina and/or Journal Jottings

The first question is a question you would likely ponder when in a guided experience of Lectio Divina. Journal writing and Lectio Divina can overlap. Some teachers and leaders will want to guide you in Lectio Divina. Others will want to fast forward to journal jottings. The first question in Journal Jottings is basically what you will be asked in a guided Lectio Divina experience.

Journal Jotting Prompts

1. What phrases in Mary's song are for you the most significant?
2. Mary and Elizabeth, both pregnant, share a joyous visit together. If you gave birth, were you blessed by a friend who was pregnant at the same time?
3. In our world in front of the text, we know that Mary will have times of sorrow in the years ahead. In your experiences have there been joyful times that bring sustaining memories when life is hard?

For Further Reflection: Mary and Elizabeth in Art

I discovered Rembrandt's painting *The Visitation* (1640) in the book *The Biblical Rembrandt: Human Painter in a Landscape of Faith*, by John I. Durham. This book deserves larger print than a footnote. The Bible was so important to Rembrandt that I think his paintings are painterly exegesis.[6]

Looking at this painting I feel the joy and excitement about Mary's arrival to visit her kinswoman, Elizabeth. Zechariah is in the doorway about to step down onto what we might call a small patio. Elizabeth and Mary are spotlighted from a softly lit cloud in the evening sky. Perhaps the moon is the source of this sublime light. A young girl helps Mary out of her heavy cloak. A little dog sniffs things out, excited to have company. Elizabeth's hand on Mary shoulder is a tender gesture of welcome. This painting expresses bonding, an ineffable experience beyond words, even poetry. Maybe Mary's pleasant time with Elizabeth, and presumable respite from waiting on Joseph freed her soul for poetic pondering.

Poetic Response to Mary's Poem: Luke 1:46–55

I treasure a small metal dish that inspired my poem based on Mary's poem.

Sermon in a Sonnet

Cherished sermon from upside down starfish
With seaweed, scallop, horn shell, and mud snail
Wreathing the rim of a cast metal dish
Like a friendly note in old fashioned mail.

Biblical verses, authored by Luke, song
From Mary's heart, upside down reversals
In God's reign where the featured poor belong,
Anticipation, a dress rehearsal.

Lowly in regard, poor in body, soul
Future justice, only in part before,
Believe we are all children in God's mold.
Faith in equality is trust restored.

6. Here are two links: rembrandtpaintings.com/the-visitation.jsp and dia.org/art/collection/object/visitation-58220.

Mary's Poem

Beautiful starfish, broken selves will mend.
Good news to send, Alleluia Amen.

Sharon R. Chace

Jesus Learns from Mother Mary

Luke 4:14–29

Reflection: Jesus Reads in the Synagogue: The Background to the Text

BOTH LUKE AND MATTHEW based their Gospels on Mark's general outline. Luke based his account of Jesus reading in the sanctuary on Mark 6:1–6. Mark was brief yet he tells us a very significant detail. Jesus taught in the synagogue. People were in one of his favorite words "astounded." Luke rounds out the story from his sources that Mark did not have. This story is Luke's signature story, which is short yet is very significant because it is a summary of the thrust of Jesus' ministry. As Warren Carter and Amy-Jill Levine state: "Indeed, many commentators take this pericope as Luke's signature scene summarizing the gospel's main points."[1] Their word "scene" suggests to me that this passage would make a good dramatic reading with scenery. Jesus announces his mission by quoting an embedded poem from the prophet Isaiah, who is frequently quoted in the New Testament.

This poem is supported by narrative. Put another way, this poem is inside prose. After Jesus was tempted in the wilderness

---

1. Carter and Levine, *New Testament*, 62.

that echoes the foundational experience of the Hebrews in the wilderness, Jesus, armed with the power of the spirit, returned to Galilee and preached in synagogues. He came to Nazareth where he had been brought up and went to the synagogue there. Leading worship in the faith community of his childhood, he opened the scroll. "The Spirit of the Lord is upon me, because he has anointed me/to bring good news to the poor. He has sent me to proclaim release to the captives/and recovery of sight to the blind, to let the oppressed go free, to proclaim the year of the Lord's favor" (Luke 4:18). This short passage captures Luke's favorite themes: A. Concern for the poor, and B. Release from captivity and oppression. Captivity comes in different forms including sin, illness, and economic bondage. Release from oppression, whether by sin or poverty or ill health, is salvation. In Luke Jesus is explicitly described as savior in Mary's poem (1:47) and the birth story (2:11).

Luke learned from his mother. Jesus' mission statement is foreshadowed by the Magnificat. In both Mary's Song and Jesus' temple reading the poor and oppressed from Hebrew Scripture are included in redemption and release.

Did Luke make up this story or did Jesus actually read that passage about his calling? I vote with some reservation that Luke's report is historically accurate. In support of facts that are close to historical, the assistant likely did not open the scroll to a prescribed passage. Jesus opened it by himself and found the passage that fueled his preaching. Generally in the Gospels Jesus is a teacher more than a preacher. Anticipating a question from the class, I emphasize that the Sermon on the Mount is not a sermon that Jesus spoke all at once but rather is a collection of his sayings that Matthew arranged from his sources. Yet in the synagogue Jesus is a preacher. The detail of finding the right place in the scroll to convey Jesus' convictions is partial evidence that Jesus preaching from Isaiah is historically accurate. However, it is important to consider the words from the late Daniel J. Harrington, SJ, with whom I studied at Weston Jesuit School of Theology. He said that biblical writers often put words into peoples' mouths that they could have or should have said. If Luke put words into Jesus' mouth or added historical fictional derails, he was in no way lying. He was telling the truth through faithful historical fiction. He stressed in the prologue, which is also a dedication to Theophilus, that he would tell the truth. Luke was not a reporter for FOX or CNN. Poetry and faithful, historical fiction in the reporting style of Luke's day was his way of conveying truth. Also Luke, who wrote excellent Koine Greek, liked to find precise words. Truth was so important to Luke that in Acts 1:3 when referring to resurrection appearances of Jesus he used a very strong Greek word for "proofs."

One historical fact is that the historical Jesus was a Jew. His sermon flowed from his heart, mind, and internalization of the Hebrew Scriptures or the Old Testament.[2] Therefore when Christians care for the poor and marginalized, their concerns are not in contrast with Judaism. Instead their caring grows out of Judaism. Luke's gift of writing opened up Jesus' ethics.

The Text: The Rejection of Jesus at Nazareth

Luke 4:14–29 contains both poetry and prose.

> When he came to Nazareth, where he had been brought up, he went to the synagogue on the sabbath day, as was his custom. He stood up to read, and the scroll of the prophet Isaiah was given to him. He unrolled the scroll and found the place where it was written . . . (Luke 4:16–17)

To repeat again out of high regard for this poem embedded in prose:

> The Spirit of the LORD is upon me,
> because he has anointed me
> to bring good news to the poor.
> He has sent me to proclaim release to the captives
> and recovery of sight to the blind,
> to let the oppressed go free,
> to proclaim the year of the LORD's favor. (Luke 4:18–19)

2. When I first wrote this, I made a typo. I wrote "glowed" instead of "flowed." The word "glowed" works emotionally. Glowing with inner light is blessing life.

The following verses are a prose conclusion that rounds out the implications of Jesus reading from Isaiah. And he rolled up the scroll, gave it back to the attendant, and sat down. The eyes of all in the synagogue were fixed on him. Then he began to say to them, "Today this scripture has been fulfilled in your hearing" (Luke 4:20–21). Isaiah's poem and Jesus' sermon-poem offer sustaining beauty for broken selves.

After the poem summarizing Jesus' calling, the narrative or story continues. The townspeople of Nazareth are angry (vv. 28–29). Interpretations vary. One angle posits that townspeople were angry not because Jesus was concerned for people outside Nazareth but because Jesus did not seem to want to share power. Yet if they had figured out that Jesus was to be a light to the gentiles as well as to Israel they could have been upset. Luke Timothy Johnson, in summary, said that the veiled intimation that the prophet would be for all people and not just for Jews could have aroused anger.[3] Well, perhaps ancient synagogues and contemporary churches are not so different. In my observation, not many people in church and society want to share power and leadership. In small-town churches, power issues are often foremost. Theological concerns at best are secondary. Put most simply, the angry townspeople of Nazareth were, in the cliché I have heard most often, "small potatoes in a small town."

Luke makes it clear that Jesus is a true prophet like Isaiah. McWhirter says, "This prophecy states everything Luke wants to convey about Jesus' mission. The Holy Spirit rests on Jesus." In summary, God has anointed Jesus with a mission to those in need. Luke's Jesus needs only to add, "Today this scripture has been fulfilled in your hearing" (4:21).[4]

To reiterate, verses 18–19 comprise the poem which is embedded in a prose introduction (vv. 14–16) and conclusion (v. 19). The poetic element that stands out is brevity. The repetition of the word "to" reinforces the sense of mission. The word "proclaim" is significant because it is related to the word "proclamation," which is a basic feature of preaching the good news of healing and salvation, which are synonymous.

3. Johnson, *Gospel of Luke*, 82.
4. McWhirter, *Rejected Prophets*, 49.

Jesus' sermon and Simeon's eyes seeing salvation for all people in tandem support the opening up of revelatory light to gentiles. Jesus' mission statement is foreshadowed by another poem inside narrative. Simeon's poem of praise in Luke (2:29–32) affirms the gentile mission as I discussed in the introduction. In summary, Simeon saw God's salvation in Jesus as a light for revelation to the gentiles. The prophet Elijah also foreshadows Luke's concern for the salvation of all. As Jocelyn McWhirter points out, God sends him to a gentile (1 Kgs 17:8–16).[5] The widow was an outsider. Therefore Elijah helps Luke's agenda of God's love opening up to all people. I picture Simeon, Isaiah, Elijah, and Jesus as soul brothers who point to the gentile mission.

Response: The World in Front of the Text: Lectio Divina and/or Journal Jottings

1. What phrases stand out to you?

2. Are the words "a light for revelation" abstract or concrete? If you are Christian does the understanding of Jesus as God incarnate suggest concrete? If you are not Christian is it possible to understand Jesus as "a light for revelation" in a more universal affirmation? Put another way: If you are a humanist is it possible to consider Jesus to be the light of the world, without believing in Christian doctrines?

3. Write about a time when you would not likely have used the word "calling" but you felt happy because of fulfilling a task or project. Name the time in your life when you felt most competent. What does that time tell you about what you think is God's will or the most logical suggestion of your present calling or activities? Was there foreshadowing by experiences earlier in your life?

4. If your life has already found you and you are doing what you are meant to do, how did you find your way?

5. McWhirter, *Rejected Prophets*, 45.

Paul Preaches in Poetry

First Corinthians 13

Reflection: General Background to First Corinthians: The First Letter to the Corinthians

First Corinthians is a letter that is part of a discussion that continues with 2 Corinthians. Paul wrote this letter around AD 54 or 55. He likely wrote from Ephesus[1] to a congregation of mostly Gentile Christians.[2] Because Paul was away, he sent correspondence to assist with the problems and divisions in the emerging church. The most serious division was between rich people and poor people (11:17–22). The sacrament we know as Communion, or the Eucharist or the Lord's Supper, was not the same for everyone. The rich ate first and the poor came later. Paul knew that Christian love means equal regard. Basically he told the rich people to eat at home if they were that hungry (11:33). The practice of speaking in tongues presented problems because some people who spoke that way thought they were better than other people. Paul stressed the variety of gifts that people offer to God (12:27–31).

1. Brown, *Introduction to the New Testament*, 512.
2. Harrington, *Who Is Jesus?*, 87.

The congregation also argued about what Christians should eat. Paul maintained that Christians could eat meat sacrificed to idols because that pagan practice was meaningless. But if others were upset, the better choice was not to eat the sacrificial meat. His slogan was "'all things are lawful,' but not all things are beneficial" (10:23). His disapproval of eating in pagan temples must have presented a bigger problem for his congregation. Not socializing with friends who did not become Christians could result in a loss of status that was very important in a society based on honor and shame, patronage and pride of place.

Warren Carter and Amy-Jill Levine examine the New Testament through various methods and meanings. In their treatment of 1 Corinthians they analyze through the lens of social-scientific criticism. The word "scientific" does not imply exact precision but rather as a general guide.[3] Social, then and now, refers to society and its customs, attitudes, values, and rules. "Negotiations around the concept of honor and shame and around patron-client structures offer insights into ways in which the church defines itself." Paul plays down the markers of his Roman society such as noble birth, wealth, and education. Instead he emphasizes commitment to a crucified lord.[4] His congregation had to give up what we call today their social support systems of meals and burial societies. Therefore, to my mind, people in the Corinthian assembly or church would need a loving community to counter isolation and loss of friendships or even family. The poetry of 1 Corinthians 13 could further the good will or Christian love (agape) in their new community of faith. Poetry can be sustaining for individuals and communities.

Background to 1 Corinthians 13

As a sermon, preacher, and teacher, Paul departs from his preferred plain speech and is eloquent. His congregation was more divided

---

3. Carter and Levine, *New Testament*, 130–31.
4. Carter and Levine, *New Testament*, 131.

than Congress in the Trump administration. The "Love Chapter" as it is sometimes called has the artistic feature of being a focal point that ties the entire book together. It is also a poetic summary of Paul's thinking about his divided congregation. In this poetic passage, Paul preached practical wisdom that could help people then and now to get along in communities. Yet there is more than practicality at work here. The words "in a mirror, dimly" suggest that beyond human sight and verbal expression there is the ineffable. Paul was not a "holier than thou" preacher. The use of the personal pronoun, "I," shows that he critiqued himself as not always loving. His gifts as well as the gifts of his talented flock would not be eternal, as would faith, hope, and love. Love is the greatest because love is the essence of God.

The Text: 1 Corinthians 13: The Gift of Love

If I speak in the tongues of mortals and of angels, but do not have love, I am a noisy gong or a clanging cymbal. And if I have prophetic powers, and understand all mysteries and all knowledge, and if I have all faith, so as to remove mountains, but do not have love, I am nothing. If I give away all my possessions, and if I hand over my body so that I may boast, but do not have love, I gain nothing.

Love is patient; love is kind; love is not envious or boastful or arrogant or rude. It does not insist on its own way; it is not irritable or resentful; it does not rejoice in wrongdoing, but rejoices in the truth. It bears all things, believes all things, hopes all things, endures all things.

Love never ends. But as for prophecies, they will come to an end; as for tongues, they will cease; as for knowledge, it will come to an end. For we know only in part, and we prophesy only in part; but when the complete comes, the partial will come to an end. When I was a child, I spoke like a child, I thought like a child, I reasoned like a child; when I became an adult, I put an end to childish ways. For now we see in a mirror, dimly, but then we will see face to face. Now I know only in part; then I will know fully, even as I have been fully known.

> And now faith, hope, and love abide, these three; and the
> greatest of these is love.

First Corinthians 13 is not indented but is a chapter in itself inserted into a book of prose. Drawing upon the thoughts of Bailey
and Vander Broek, I consider the poetic repetition of the word
"if." Feel the flow and rhythm as the poem builds. Think how flat
verse 1 would be in declarative prose sentences. Look at the first
line as prose: Without love I am nothing. That declarative sentence
is no match for "If I speak in the tongues of mortals and of angels,
but do not have love, I am a noisy gong or a clanging cymbal."
   According to scholars James L. Bailey and Lyle D. Vander
Broek, 1 Corinthians 13 is written in a poetic form called a chi-
asm. Its most important characteristic is a reverse parallelism
where phrases are stated in basically a reverse order. Here is their
diagram of 1 Corinthians 13:

A. Love never ends.

   B. But as for prophecies, they will come to an end;

      as for tongues, they will cease;

      as for knowledge, it will come to an end.

      C. For we know only in part,

         and we prophesy only in part;

         but when the complete comes,

         the partial will come to an end.

         D. When I was a child,

            I spoke like a child.

            I thought like a child.

            I reasoned like a child,

            when I became an adult, I put an end to childish

            ways.

      C'. For now we see in a mirror, dimly,

         but then we will see face to face.

         Now I know only in part;

         then I will know fully, even as I have been fully

         known.

B'. And now faith, hope, and love abide, these three;
A'. and the greatest of these is love.[5]

As Bailey and Vander Broek go on to note: C and C' are parallel elements. C' introduces the image of the mirror and thus adds meaning to C. B and B' are contrasting. In my view biblical exegetes and poets seeing connections is part of their work. The diagram adds to interpreting because the contrasts of gifts connects chapter 13 with chapter 12, which describes the various kinds of gifts given by the Spirit through which people serve the church. However, all these gifts pale compared to the excellent way of love in chapter 13.

The word "love" is an abstract noun. Clergy might want to consider connecting this Christian love poem with other biblical passages that actualize love. For example, the story of the Good Samaritan comes to mind. Another possibility is to think about how the gifts of parishioners participate in Christian love. Gifts might be the ones that Paul identified or gifts can be understood more broadly. As an artist and poet I offer caution. Discernment of love in art and writing is not as easy as seeing love in social service. Poetry and art can offer sustenance, beauty and truth. Love is in the process. Perhaps the humanities are God's auxiliary.

However, scholars do not always agree about what is and what is not poetry. Amos N. Wilder, who I deeply respect, did not think that the love chapter is a poem. While on the one hand, he saw rhythm as a marker of poetry, "The one test that we can rely on will be that of rhythm,"[6] yet he did not see the love chapter as poetry. "Paul's hymn to love in 1 Corinthians is rhythmic indeed, but we would not count it as poetry."[7] I wonder if the disagreement is a matter of generational sensibilities with younger scholars being more open to a wider definition of poetry. Wilder's book was published in 1964. Bailey and Vander Broek were published in 1992.

Does the term "prose poem" work? The brief definition in the Merriam Webster online dictionary is "a composition in prose that

5. Bailey and Vander Broek, *Literary Forms in the New Testament*, 49–53.

6. Wilder, *Language of the Gospels*, 100.

7. Wilder, *Language of the Gospels*, 115.

has some of the qualities of a poem." I think that definition works as one description of the love chapter. Ambiguity is not the enemy in literary discussions.

Response: The World in Front of the Text

1. What phrases stand out to you?

2. Is there a phrase that suggests something that you need to work on?

3. If you have heard this chapter multiple times, does it grow in importance or lose freshness?

4. If it is no longer fresh, how can it become as new to you again?

5. Do you in any way identify with your faith being countercultural?

6. Have poems, either religious or secular, sustained you?

Poet-Hymn of Essence and Exaltation

Philippians 2:1–11

Reflection: The General Background

WRITTEN AROUND 56 AD to Paul's first church or assembly, Philippians is a letter with the customary greeting, body, and closing benediction. Even though Paul writes from prison, Philippians is a remarkably happy book. Ever thankful to God and his people, Paul is upbeat. Being in prison is a situation that helps Paul to spread the gospel. The Philippians are true friends. Being a true friend was a virtue in Roman society and in Paul's churches. As Warren Carter and Amy-Jill Levine point out, the hallmarks of friendship were honored in the Roman world of Paul's day. A person's usefulness, ability to be good company, and shared values contributed to friendship among the elite. Among people who were not social equals there could be mutual support usually in the form of patron-client relationships.[1] Paul modifies that approach by asking his parishioners to not pay him or treat him like a patron. Instead the risen Christ is the patron and Paul the slave or servant. This reversal of obligation is a theological and social achievement, a breakthrough to deeper participation in Christ.

1. Carter and Levine, *New Testament*, 201.

Thinking positively about his flock, Paul prays that their love will overflow with knowledge and full insight. (1:9). In contrast to the calm reasoning in Romans, Paul writes emotionally with affection. Therefore it is possible that the rough transitions between parts in the body are a result of passionate, flowing thought with emotional rather than logical ordering. Yet the letter may be a compilation of two or three Pauline letters. Compilation would explain why the thank-you note is at the end rather than the more likely beginning of a letter. We cannot know everything about Paul's situation, but he may have thanked the Philippians on a previous occasion for their gift so he did not need to mention it first in his letter. Whether this letter was written all at once or compiled from shorter pieces, Philippians is a letter of joy and thanksgiving that is best read as a unified piece. This joy-filled letter stresses rejoicing, unity in community, sharing in the mind of Christ through service, and openness to sacramental suffering. Fidelity in relationship to God and gentleness in human relationships are guiding ideals.

Philippians 2:1–11: The Background to the Text of the Poem-Hymn

Christians participate in the life of Christ or live out the life of Christ by following his example of obedience and humble service. The idea of living like Christ is woven through the New Testament and comes to fullest expression in Philippians. This passage is a prayer, poem, and hymn inserted in Paul's letter to the Philippians. The first person to note that this pericope predated Paul was Ernst Lohmeyer, about ninety years ago.[2] It is unlikely that Paul wrote the entire hymn because this poem-hymn is written in better Koine Greek than the Greek that Paul wrote. He probably knew the hymn and quoted it from Christian worship. Therefore it tells us something about early Christian beliefs about Jesus. An important theological point is that this hymn shows that at an early stage Christians understood Jesus as sharing God's form. Yet Jesus did not exploit his relationship with God as the poet-writer understood. The historical context adds to

2. Marchal, "Expecting a Hymn, Encountering an Argument," 246.

our understanding. Philippi was an administration center for the government. Serf farmers in the surrounding farmlands produced crops that benefitted the Roman government. In contrast to Jesus in the "Christ Hymn" who did not claim equality with God as something to grasp, the Roman emperor has no trouble proclaiming himself to be God.

Many Christians see this passage as a statement of Christ's preexistence with God. Understanding of Jesus as the new Adam is another perspective that is growing on me. Others stress Jesus taking the form of a servant like the suffering servant in Isaiah. That was my view for years and still is in part. Yet I see the loopholes. In Isaiah the servant is Israel, not an individual. Plus serving was an honor rather than degradation.[3] Not everyone is called to suffer "even death on a cross." The word "even" suggests that death by crucifixion is not the norm. Therefore suffering, although part of life, was not in itself glorified in the Isaiah passage nor the only outcome of service as it is in the thinking of many Protestants in Puritan traditions, both religious and secular. To counterbalance the too neat equation of suffering and service, Joseph A. Marchal discusses a mythic interpretation. In this perspective, "the hymn narrates an event of mythic proportions," and then descent into the word and ascent into heavenly exaltation.[4] This is a hard event to follow, hence no pressure to completely imitate.

Jesus as the new Adam might converge with the concept of myth because the emphasis, or so it seems to me, is more about salvation and somewhat less on ethics of imitation. Christ in this passage as the new Adam seems logical and my idea of reversed typology, a story of sin and reversal. Adam made mistakes, wanting to essentially be God rather than settling for being made in the image of God. But Jesus did not exploit his divine nature. Following his example of not being concerned by status can help people participate in holy living. Service can take precedent over status. Finding joy in one's calling is valuable. Suffering is not the whole story. A bridge-building implication is that following one's calling in obedience to

3. Hooker, "Letter to the Philippians," 503.
4. Marchal, "Expecting a Hymn, Encountering an Argument," 247.

God or a person's best discernment is more important than status. Trust comes before obedience to inner promptings or conviction of God's call. Jesus trusted God enough to obey the call of his heavenly Father. Trusting in life or in God is necessary in order to follow your path of service. Doing what a person feels called to do is to claim one's essence even if society demeans the choice. Exaltation comes through achievement of personal best in service or devotion. Sometimes there is earthly recognition. In any case, one may feel God saying, "Well done, good slave" (Luke 19:17).

Walter Brueggemann stresses Jesus' obedience and therefore not being grasping or greedy for power. Jesus emptied himself from those worldly temptations. Brueggemann states: "Following the way of the early church, Paul must resort to lyrical articulation to speak of Jesus' gift. Paul finally must offer poetry that bespeaks a reality the world cannot contain."[5] Therefore, in my view, poetry can inform ethics.

Other Perspectives

Part of the fun of biblical studies is reading other points of view. Studying different angles and interpretation is what poets in discussion group do. Of course in this book about embedded poems, I emphasize the "Christ Hymn." Apparently I am not alone in focusing on this hymn/poem. The title of the essay "Expecting a Hymn, Encountering an Argument: Introducing the Rhetoric of Philippians and Pauline Interpretation" by Joseph A. Marchal signals a literary approach.

Two concerns in his essay are most significant in my way of thinking. Firstly, it is important to note that taking on the nature of a slave was a free choice for Paul. Slaves in Philippi did not have a choice. Hopefully they knew about Paul's feelings in his greeting: "Paul and Timothy, servants of Christ Jesus" (1:1). Not only for the servants or slaves in Paul's time, but in centuries following, it would be important to not glorify servant hood or slavery.

---

5. Brueggemann, *Finally Comes the Poet,* 108.

Secondly the issue of obedience as well as having sacred merit might have a down side. Paul looks at Jesus' obedience as a model for himself. The ethical implication of friendship as care for others is most laudable. However, even saints including Paul might have mixed motives. Paul seems to want his flock to obey him. In 2:12 he says to his beloved, "just as you have always obeyed me." As you know from my treatment of Luke, I have a hermeneutic of suspicion about leaders and power issues.

Whether or not you take seriously the thought of Ralph P. Martin, his thinking demonstrates parallelism as an underlying form. He considered three phrases to be Paul's addition to this Christological hymn: "even death on a cross" (2:8); "in heaven and on earth and under the earth" (2:3); and "to the glory of God, the Father" (2:11).[6] These verses do seem to me to be tacked on but in a more positive note, Paul's way of rounding out the hymn by developing the implications of his inherited hymn. Without these verses the parallelism is clear.

> who, though he was in the form of God,
> did not regard equality with God
> as something to be exploited,
>
> but emptied himself,
> taking the form of a slave,
> being born in human likeness,
>
> And being found in human form,
> he humbled himself
> and became obedient to the point of death—
>
> Therefore God also highly exalted him,
> and gave him the name
> that is above every name,
>
> so that at the name of Jesus
> every knee should bend,
> and every tongue should confess
> that Jesus Christ is Lord.

6. Bailey and Vander Broek, *Literary Forms in the New Testament*, 80.

Let us look at the passage as in appears in its entirety and consider the poetic elements.

> Let the same mind be in you that was in Christ Jesus,
> who, though he was in the form of God,
> did not regard equality with God
> as something to be exploited,
> but emptied himself,
> taking the form of a slave,
> being born in human likeness.
> And being found in human form,
> he humbled himself
> and became obedient to the point of death—
> even death on a cross.
> Therefore God also highly exalted him
> and gave him the name
> that is above every name,
> so that at the name of Jesus
> every knee should bend,
> in heaven and on earth and under the earth,
> and every tongue should confess
> that Jesus Christ is LORD,
> to the glory of God the Father. (Phil 2:5–11, NRSV)

Poets evolve. Changes are part of the creative process in an individual's writing life or in the life of faith communities when, for example, the words of a hymn are changed in order to use more inclusive language. So if words were added that make parallelism harder to spot, you may feel that the possible additions detract or on the other hand develop meanings. The important question then and now is: Do changes serve the church or community in their basic mission to help and heal? In any case, considering the development of a poem can add to appreciation of the creative process of individual authors, editors, redactors, and the spiritual needs of communities.

So let us consider the poetic elements of rhythm, words, and movement. Feel the hymn-like rhythm. To claim beat would be an overstatement. Yet there is a balanced cadence in lines of similar length. Think about key words. Often the word "and" is considered to be a weak word. Yet in this the word "and" moves the poem along, building the author's case that Jesus is a spiritual Lord, even more important than the Emperor. Another key word that is a turning point in the poem/ hymn is "therefore." After experiencing humbling and being obedient and dying on the cross, therefore God gave Jesus a name that is above other names such as the title "Emperor." Jesus did not exploit that claim.

This poetic device marks a significant ontological change in status. Status was understood in the ancient world as shame and honor. Status is still connected to shame. I worry especially about young people. Consider the power of fat-shaming to lower a person's feelings of worthiness or being arty in a high school that favors athletes.

Whatever one's perspective there can be agreement that this prayer is about essence and exaltation. An important word is "therefore." This word marks the transition from the essence of humble service to exaltation in God. Transition is movement, a poetic quality.

Response: The World in Front of the Text: Lectio Divina and/or Journal Jottings

If your pastor or teacher wants to lead you in Lectio Divina stop here. Writing in your journal could also follow Lectio Divina.

If you prefer to forgo Lectio Divina to write in your journal proceed to the questions.

1. What phrases stand out to you?

2. Why are these phrases important for you?

3. How is it possible to live a Christlike life as an individual or in community?

4. Obedience is a difficult concept: Consider obedience as a personal sense of your calling, a biblical imperative, or a communal vision. What do you think?

For Further Study: Painterly Exegesis

George Rouault like Jesus cared for people who are poor and live on the margins. He explored the implications of this hymn-poem in his art. His print titled *Obedient unto Death, Even the Death of the Cross* shows a peaceful and trusting Jesus.

Rouault's painting *Christ in the Outskirts* suggests both prophetic critique and hope. (You can find both images with an Internet search.) *Christ in the Outskirts* seems more desolate than Edward Hopper's most somber paintings. Christ and three children stand together in a street scene that seems like a bombed-out city. You can feel the caring of Jesus. A critique of a world where the powerful cast the poor away is one message. Another interpretation is that there is hope in the implicit invitation for people to have the mind that was in Jesus. The moon shines on Jesus the Christ, suggesting that Christ is the light of the world. Rouault's images encourage lives of trying and trusting, caring and sharing.

A Short Sketch of William Blake

William Blake was born in London in 1757 and died in 1827. He attended art schools, including the Royal Academy. Even as a child he wrote some poetry. At age fourteen he was apprenticed as an engraver. As an adult he was an engraver, painter, poet, and visionary. He colored his etchings often with the help of his understanding wife, Catherine. Blake's poems and etchings were often based on the Bible. Because he was a visionary he was the right person to create the colored engraving *Death on a Pale Horse*, which is included in the section on Revelation in volume 12 of *The New Interpreter's Bible* (based on Rev 19:11–21).

As a poet, Blake envisioned a universal humanity. In his view people can partake of God's nature. Therefore people and God are connected. Describing his purpose Blake wrote:

> To open the immortal Eyes
> Of man inwards into the worlds of thought; into Eternity
> Ever expanding in the Bosom of God, the Human
> Imagination.

Another Poem by William Blake

Paul and William Blake were very different people. Yet it seems to me that a poem by William Blake titled "The Divine Image" can help us answer Paul's prayer that his current readers grow in love and insight. Having the same mind that was in Christ Jesus is heightened aspiration and maybe was challenging even for Blake.

The Divine Image

To Mercy, Pity, Peace, and Love
All pray in their distress;
And to these virtues of delight
Return their thankfulness.

For Mercy, Pity, Peace, and Love
Is God, our father dear,
And Mercy, Pity, Peace, and Love
Is Man, his child and care.

For Mercy has a human heart,
Pity a human face,
And Love, the human form divine,
And Peace, the human dress.

Then every man, of every clime,
That prays in his distress,
Prays to the human form divine,
Love, Mercy, Pity, Peace.

And all must love the human form,
In heathen, Turk, or Jew;
Where Mercy, Love, and Pity dwell
There God is dwelling too.

Continuity of a Blessing

Numbers 6:22–26

Reflection: The Background

THE MOST WELL-KNOWN BLESSING in this chapter is the priestly blessing in Numbers 6:24–26, written during Israel's time in the wilderness. It is a priestly blessing that is a conclusion to the laws of defilement. Although strange to us today, the rules helped keep the people of the tent community healthy. The priest blesses the community by assuring his people of God's blessing at the close of worship. At that time the blessing was perceived to have almost magical power. Notice that verses 22 and 23 are prose and part of the storyline that introduces the poem.

The blessing in Numbers is a polished, liturgical blessing that transcends its time and original situation. The person presiding asks for God's blessing then and now. A most important word is "peace." Various connotations in addition to the absence of war are good health, security, and wellness. This blessing continues to be used at the conclusion of worship services.

Continuity of a Blessing

Numbers 6:22–26

Introductory verses to the blessing

The LORD spoke to Moses, saying: Speak to Aaron and his sons, saying, Thus you shall bless the Israelites: You shall say to them, (vv. 22–23)

The Blessing

The LORD bless you and keep you;
the LORD make his face to shine upon you,
and be gracious to you;
the LORD lift up his countenance upon you, and give you peace.
(vv. 24–26)

Important features of this benediction are brevity and, as we have seen, a long shelf life spanning centuries and diverse faith communities. Although interfaith friendly because this blessing is beloved by both Christians and Jews, this blessing is not universal, yet at the same time veers in that direction. The verses are short declarative sentences which move the blessing along. Verbs are powerful: "bless," "make," and "lift." Maybe you could write your own poem using those three words. Are there universal aspects to these words? Have you had an experience of God's face shining upon you that gives lasting, almost indescribable joy?

Other Blessings and Benedictions

There is ongoing holiness in continuing to bless. Biblical blessings come in poetic fragments. Benedictions are blessings. Blessings can also be greetings. There is a bit of mix and match. Benedictions praise God and give believers strength. Greetings ask for God's blessings and are at the start of letters. Benedictions are at the end. Therefore, technically, they are not embedded nor inserted. Yet they function as prayer-poems that introduce or conclude narratives or letters. You can look them up in your Bibles and if there is time and people have different versions you can compare translations. In a class short passages are well-suited for comparisons.

Greetings

> 1 Cor 1:3
>
> 2 Thess 1:2
>
> Jude 1:2

Benedictions

> 2 Cor 13:13
>
> Phil 4:23
>
> Jude 1:24–25

Years ago I heard selected phrases from the benediction in Jude. This benediction was (paraphrasing): "Now to him who is able to keep you from falling be glory, majesty, and power forever. Amen." The reason I remember this more than sixty years later is that, having coordination issues, I fell frequently. Seems to me that the combination of praising God and affirming God's strength to keep us from falling on many levels—mine literal, Jude's falling away from faith and falling into licentious behavior—is empowering.

The World in Front of the Text: Lectio Divina and/or Journal Jottings

Listen to this priestly benediction and blessing in Numbers 6:22–26 again. Hear the poetic rhythm of the repeated phrase "The Lord."

Response: Journal Jottings

Questions to prompt journal writings and discussion

1. What words or phrases stand out for you?
2. Do you feel empowered by the benediction in your church? Why or why not?

3. What helps you to bless life?

4. Do you want to write a benediction?

A Concluding Benediction

Let us end this session with a benediction written by Paul in 2 Corinthians. I chose this blessing because it is the one I used at the conclusions of my classes in the Greek New Testament at First Congregational Church in Rockport, Massachusetts.

"The grace of the Lord Jesus Christ, the love of God, and the communion of the Holy Spirit be with all of you" (2 Cor 13:13).

For Further Reflection

There are several poems or songs in Numbers. The following three biblical poems condense important spiritual experiences. Even the war poem is not overly gory. The titles are mine.

- A Song of Israel Winning in Battles: 21:27–30
- A Song of God Providing Lifesaving Water: 21:17–18
- In Praise of Moses as the Greatest Prophet: 12:6–8

My poem expresses best wishes for readers in any faith tradition.

Greetings

May each seeker find a greeter
and with the passing of peace
intuit welcome.
At the portal of the holy,
open door is invitation
to rest and rejoice in:
the beauty of holiness,
the beauty of color,
the beauty of light,
the realm of God.

I wrote the following benediction for my family to use if they wish to do so at my memorial service. You, my readers, are invited to use or share.

Benediction

God's peace will sustain you on your walk into ongoing life. Go forth, trusting that "joy comes in the morning." Amen.

SESSION 7

Sharing Journal Jottings and/or Writing a Group Poem

Suggestions

DEPENDING UPON THE NUMBER of participants, ask each person who wants to share his or her journal jottings to speak for five to seven minutes. Journal notes might articulate insights about biblical poems or fresh knowledge of selves. Literature can inform people about human nature and be a source of strength, even spiritual formation.

Or, if people want to create a group poem, ask each participant to write approximately seven words about themselves or insights from their journals. Make a list poem of the phrases. The order can be random or fall into categories if the person in charge of compiling sees phrases that are related. The compiler may be anyone among the group.

Inspiration from biblical parallelism: Consider couplets with two lines that are similar or two lines that differ, or two lines that for any reason seem to go well together. Lines do not need to be complete sentences. No need to be rigid about the fit on two lines. If seven words are too long for one line, just indent extra words below. If people wish, their name could be at the start. Here is an example. Sharon: Painterly poet, savoring stillness.

After the poem is complete ask someone to write a prose introduction about the poem. A prose conclusion is also a possibility. Therefore the finished product is a poem inside prose.

If the compiler needs to work on the poem after the class, consider having a second session to talk and celebrate the artistry of journals and/or group poem.

Epilogue

God as Just Judge and Poet-Prophet

The Back Story

A MIXED METAPHOR FOR God as just judge and poet-prophet is embedded in prayer—poems throughout the Bible. Poems and prayers are intertwined. I discovered this mixed metaphor, which is a derivative biblical image of God, during a discussion segment in a course called Prayer in the Bible, taught by John S. Kselman at Weston Jesuit School of Theology, now School of Theology and Ministry, at Boston College. An earlier version of this essay was published in my book, *Protestant Pulse: Heart Hopes for God*. At that time I had not found the book, *Finally Comes the Poet: Daring Speech for Proclamation*, by Walter Brueggemann. Therefore references to his book are additions to my first essay. It is important for me to note additions because they show the development of my thinking over decades. I seldom get to where I am headed all at once. While writing this book, guided by intuition and quite possibly subconscious remembering, I reread 1 and 2 Samuel. I wondered why I had not discussed the double metaphor in David's last words (2 Sam 23:1–7).

Synopsis

1. The mixed metaphor of God as a just judge and poet-prophet is woven throughout the Bible, often in embedded prayer poems.

2. The derivative image of God as a just judge with a poet's heart and a prophet's voice first appears in the Bible in Gen 15:1–21.

3. If the Bible is understood as divinely inspired, biblical poetry reflects God's voice and suggests that God is a poet.

4. God is ultimately beyond all metaphors including just judge and poet-prophet.

God as Just Judge and Poet-Prophet

The double metaphor of just judge and poet-prophet is summarized in Genesis 15:1–6.

> After these things the word of the Lord came to Abram in a vision, "Do not be afraid, Abram, I am your shield; your reward shall be very great." But Abram said, "O Lord God, what will you give me, for I continue childless, and the heir of my house is Eliezer of Damascus?" And Abram said, "You have given me no offspring, and so a slave born in my house is to be my heir." But the word of the Lord came to him, "This man shall not be your heir; no one but your very own issue shall be your heir." He brought him outside and said, "Look toward heaven and count the stars, if you are able to count them." Then he said to him, "So shall your descendants be." And he believed the Lord; and the Lord reckoned it to him as righteousness.

These verses suggest complementary dimensions of God as just judge and poet-prophet. As judge, God assesses Abram and justly reckons his faith as righteousness (15:6). Speaking poetically, God reassures Abram about his prophetic mission to procreate. God in poet mode uses words metaphorically. Shield is a metaphor for protection. The stars in the sky symbolize the many descendants that will come from Abram. Put another way: If the "Word of the Lord" comes through the words of men then God's poetic words as imagined by the biblical authors suggests that God is a poet.

In Genesis God as a just judge is a concept that emphasizes dialogue. Charged with the responsibilities of instructing the people of Israel in the ways of righteousness and justice (Gen 18:19), Abram, now Abraham, similarly dares to hold God, who might sweep away the righteous with the wicked, to the same requirements." Speaking up in the lament tradition Abraham asks: "Shall not the Judge of all the earth do what is just?" (Gen 18:25).[1] Thus God and Abraham are partners in conversation. They talk to one another. Walter Brueggemann points out that Robert Alter speaks about "the quintessential biblical notice of the nexus of speech that bonds God and human creatures."[2] Conversation, as a bond, suggests that God is not so above the human race that he cannot be questioned. Nor is humanity so subservient that people are not permitted to think for themselves.

In the Bible prayer is conversation with God. Not all readers of this book will believe in God. Therefore I offer the possibility of an atheistic version of prayer and thoughts about the poetic writing process as akin to prayer. In his book, *Prayer in the New Testament*, Oscar Cullmann condensed the thinking of Dorothy Solle's thoughts on atheistic prayer as talking to oneself.[3] One does not have to agree with her in order to ponder the implications of her definition of prayer for poetry in general. My sense is that poets often talk to themselves when thinking and writing. Their distillations and revelation to themselves through writing come from a meditative process akin to prayer. Poetry may well be the form of writing that is most like prayer.

Abraham was a believer trusting in his father God. His trust enabled him to glimpse the images of God as judge softened by

1. Balentine, *Prayer in the Hebrew Bible*, 196.
2. Brueggemann, *Finally Comes the Poet*, 49.
3. Cullmann, *Prayer in the New Testament*, 6.

God having a poet's heart. Poet God can embrace ambiguity, engage in dialogue, and at the same time speak in a prophet's voice.

By listening to Abraham's pleas God proves his ability to consider ambiguity. He can be persuaded. In 1995 at a conference about fundamentalisms at Episcopal Divinity School, I asked Dr. Martin E. Marty if there are any fundamentalists who are good poets. In summary he said that he was glad I asked because it was an issue he wanted to address. He added that fundamentalists are not good poets because they cannot handle ambiguity. However he did state that evangelicals can write good poetry. In Genesis 18, God does not reject the give-and-take of dialogue. Listening to people, contemplating many angles, posing questions to oneself, and engaging in ongoing discussion are abilities that skillful poets and seasoned journalists develop.

There is some evidence that the ability to handle ambiguity was valued in the ancient world. Being comfortable with the complexities of parables is a characteristic of scribes as described in the book of Sirach, which is one of the seven books of the Apocrypha. In Sirach's view scribes are discerning because scribes seek out the hidden meanings of proverbs and are at home with the obscurities of parables (Sir 39:3). Jesus was a speaker, not a scribe. Yet a case can be made that he was comfortable with ambiguity. The parables can be ambiguous. The author of John's Gospel implies that at one time Jesus spoke in metaphors or similes. "I have said these things to you in figures of speech. The hour is coming when I will no longer speak to you in figures, but will tell you plainly of the Father" (16:25). The New Testament Greek word for "figures" can also be translated as "similitudes."

The Bible is partly written in poetry. Poetic structure is most evident in various prophets, *Psalms*, *Proverbs*, and *Song of Solomon*. Amos N. Wilder noted that the Old Testament books most quoted in the New Testament are books of poetry, *Isaiah*, and the *Psalms*.[4] Robert Lowth's series of published Oxford lectures captured the imagination of his contemporary and subsequent biblical scholars. Ralph Waldo Emerson read this mid-eighteenth-century

4. Wilder, *Language of the Gospels*, 101.

writer, and pointed out that words for "poet" and "prophet" are the same in Hebrew.[5] Lowth's claim is that biblical prophecy was itself a form of poetry that was inspired by the Holy Spirit.[6] As we have discussed in response to the troublesome issue of Hebrew meter, he suggested "parallelism," a literary form discussed in greater detail elsewhere in this book.

A time-honored definition of "prophet" that eschews yet does not negate a predictive role is "spokesperson for God" like a messenger to a king. "We have not listened to your servants the prophets, who spoke in your name to our king, our princes, and our ancestors, and to all the people of the land" (Dan 9:6). When prophets as God's spokespersons speak in poetry, God's voice comes through evocative images. As we have seen, Brueggemann values the thinking of magisterial Roman Catholic scholar, Hans Urs von Balthasar, who said, "God needs prophets in order to make himself known, and all prophets are necessarily artistic. What a prophet has to say can never be said in prose."[7]

How did people of Israel understand the connection between prophet and poet?

James L. Kugel, in a book he edited, *Poetry and Prophecy: The Beginning of a Literary Tradition*, addresses that question in his essay, "Poets and Prophets." In brief, he said that in the eyes of early Judaism and the classic rabbinical writings, from the second to sixth century CE, song was clearly thought secondary to prophecy. There was little interest in poetic structure.[8]

However, in late Antiquity, Philo of Alexandria, the great expositor of Hebrew Scripture, said Moses learned rhythm and meter from the Egyptians. About a century later the Jewish historian, Josephus, compared David to Greek canons of poetry.[9]

Similarly Greek influence brought an understanding of the writer who was so possessed by the muse that writing came easily.

5. Richardson, *Emerson*, 12.
6. Kugel, *Poetry and Prophecy*, 22.
7. Brueggemann, *Finally Comes the Poet*, 4.
8. Kugel, *Poetry and Prophecy*, 11.
9. Kugel, *Poetry and Prophecy*, 12.

In this vein of thought Philo wrote: "For prophets are interpreters of God." Commenting on Genesis 15:12, which describes the sun going down and a deep sleep falling upon Abraham, Philo wrote, "'When the light of God shines, the human light sets; when the divine light sets, the human dawns and rises. This is what regularly befalls the fellowship of prophets. The mind is evicted at the arrival of the divine Spirit, but when that departs the mind returns to its tenancy.'"[10]

Centuries later a similar kind of inspiration was attributed to Jesus. In a romantic mode of thought, which values originality and inspiration, William Whallon made a case for Jesus as a poet. His argument was not based on parallelism but on the inspired, unique sayings of Jesus passed on by oral tradition.[11]

Jesus' teaching of the Lord's Prayer suggests interaction with God who is just judge and poet-prophet. My sense is that when people pray the Lord's Prayer in church or in private devotions there is a feeling that God is on our side. A God on our side connotes justice tempered by consideration of the human predicaments of sin and sorrow. A note of compassionate judgement comes through the Lord's Prayer as set forth by P. S. Cameron in his article, "Lead Us Not into Temptation." He concludes that the meaning of the sixth petition is "Do not judge us according to our deserts; do not bring us to open court where the verdict would be inevitable."[12] In other words, keep us away from courts where judges have already made up their minds. God, for whom verdicts are not inevitable, is a just judge with a poet prophet's ability to deal with ambiguity. Thus Jesus instructs us to pray to God, our heavenly Father, who is a just judge and poet-prophet. In Jesus' prayer, masculine description of God as Father need not limit our understanding of God because women as well as men, mothers as well as fathers, can be just judges and poet-prophets.

If a person believes that the Bible is the inspired prophetic word of God and has also noted that the Bible is part poetry, then

---

10. Kugel, *Poetry and Prophecy*, 16.

11. Whallon, *Formula, Character, and Context*, 193–208.

12. Cameron, "Lead Us Not into Temptation," 299–301.

seeing attributes of poet and prophet in God's nature is logical. Since God speaks in poetry though prophets and Jesus, God is a poet. Put another way if "The Word of the Lord" comes through the words of men, then their poetic words suggest that in their imaginations God spoke in poetry.

The definition of poetry in *Literary Forms In The New Testament: A Handbook* by James L. Bailey and Lyle D. Vander Broek provides a working definition of poetry. "Although poetry has evolved over the years, it is quite possible to give a general definition of the form that applies to both first-century and modern expressions. Two elements are central. Firstly, poetry often employs what is called figurative language." Instead of directly stating "the thoughts she or he wishes to convey, the poet uses word pictures, images, symbols, metaphors and so forth, to encourage the reader to wrestle creatively with the issues at hand." Secondly there is sustained rhythm.[13]

Was musician, poem, and songwriter David a poet-prophet and just judge? There is some biblical and scholarly evidence to say "reservedly likely." In his chapter "David the Prophet" James K. Kugel says that whatever the case David is certainly presented in prophetic language. Calling David for one example "anointed" might have encouraged seeing David as a prophet.[14] Kugel goes on to note David's words, "The spirit of the Lord speaks through me."

Not unlike Moses' song to the Lord in Exodus 15, in 2 Samuel 22 David thanks God in poetry for his victories. This poem-prayer is a summary of David's triumphs that God's power made possible. Neither Moses' poem-song nor David's has the double metaphor of just judge and poet-prophet yet both deserve mention as poems that are embedded in narratives. A more sublime poem follows in 2 Samuel 23. My sense is that designating David's last words as an oracle and saying that he is anointed in addition to David's experience that the Spirit of the Lord speaks through him suggests a poet-prophet (2 Sam 23: 1–2). In poetic fashion God is metaphorically depicted as "The Rock of Israel" (2 Sam 23:3). God is also described

---

13. Bailey and Broek, *Literary Forms in the New Testament*, 76.
14. Kugel, *Poetry and Prophecy*, 48–49.

as judging justly. Second Samuel 23:3 describes the one who rules over people justly. The pericope follows (2 Sam 23:2–7):

> Now these are the last words of David:
> The oracle of David, son of Jesse,
> the oracle of the man whom God exalted,
> the anointed of the God of Jacob,
> the favorite of the Strong One of Israel:
>
> The Last Words of David
> The spirit of the LORD speaks through me,
> his word is upon my tongue.
> The God of Israel has spoken,
> the Rock of Israel has said to me:
> One who rules over people justly,
> ruling in the fear of God,
> is like the light of morning,
> like the sun rising on a cloudless morning,
> gleaming from the rain on the grassy land.
> Is not my house like this with God?
> For he has made with me an everlasting covenant,
> ordered in all things and secure.
> Will he not cause to prosper
> all my help and my desire?
> But the godless are all like thorns that are thrown away;
> for they cannot be picked up with the hand;
> to touch them one uses an iron bar
> or the shaft of a spear.
> And they are entirely consumed in fire on the spot.

Embedded prayer in Jeremiah reveals Jeremiah and God as poets in conversation.

In Jeremiah 11:20, Jeremiah addresses God. "But you, O Lord of hosts, who judge righteously, who try the heart and the mind, let me see your retribution upon them, for to you I have committed my cause." Whether these are Jerimiah's exact words or not, they certainly convey Jeremiah's complaint about his opponents through poetry. I think that the not-so-obvious treasure in this verse is the echo of God as a just judge with a poet's heart. Jeremiah's prayer reveals conviction that the Lord judges righteously and tries the heart and mind. Good judges discern fairly. Poets can test hearts and find the pulse beats. Like Abraham, Jeremiah as poet dares to think for himself. He questions the prevailing assumption that bad people suffer and the righteous prospers. "Why do all who are treacherous thrive?" (Jer 12:1). Furthermore God knows both Jeremiah's opponents and Jeremiah himself. "But you, O Lord, know me; You see me and test me—my heart is with you" (Jer 12:3). Jeremiah, as poet prophet, is united with God through shared attributes and mission. A poet-prophet, who dares to question, will not buy the Deuteronomist's hard line, that suffering is always the result of sin.

Jeremiah's prayer sketches a verbal picture of God as a poet whose words Jeremiah relished. "Your words were found, and I ate them, and your words became to me a joy and the delight of my heart; for I am called by your name, O Lord, God of hosts" (Jer 15:16). God in turn calls Jeremiah to the responsibility to use words well. "If you utter what is precious, and not what is worthless, you shall serve as my mouth. It is they, who will turn to you, not you who will turn to them" (Jer 15:19). By implication only good poets get to be prophets. God stresses the power of persuasion: "They will turn to you." Strong persuasive ability from worthwhile words and God's presence will create strength to lead. "And I will make you to this people a fortified wall of bronze; they will fight against you, but they shall not prevail over you, for I am with you to save you and deliver you, says the Lord" (Jer 15:20).

Samuel Ballentine, in the 1993 Fortress Press edition of his book, *Prayer in the Hebrew Bible: The Drama of Divine—Human Dialogue*, states that prayers in the lament tradition that articulate undeserved suffering are predominately displayed in the poetry of the Hebrew Bible.[15]

Therefore, I delved into one of my favorite Hebrew Bible or Old Testament prophets, Habakkuk. Chapters 1 and 2 are prayerful laments in poems that challenge God. Thus Habakkuk is both part of the lament tradition and the prophetic tradition of protesting injustice. Life is not going rightly. The wicked prosper. The

---

15. Ballentine, *Prayer in the Hebrew Bible*, 118.

righteous suffer. In his opening sentence Habakkuk gets right to the point. "O Lord, how long shall I cry for help, and you will not listen?" (Hab 1:2). In 2:1 Habakkuk keeps watch for what God will say. Lo and behold, God calls Habakkuk to be a writer. "Then the Lord read it" (Hab 2:2). The runner who is like a power hiker building up speed needs to see the vision. Like Burma Shave signs of times past the message can be broken down into short phrases on individual signs seen from the road. If you are too young to remember Burma Shave signs, you can have fun looking them up on the Internet. They delivered the message, over time, in rhyme!

God Will . . .

Still . . .

Promises Keep . . .

Enemies Sleep . . .

Burma Shave.

Another view is that the messengers of God should spread the word of God's future vindication and really run with the message. Despite misfortunes Habakkuk comes to awe in the Lord's work (Hab 3:2) and trust that God is his strength (Hab 3:19).

Habakkuk complains about the proud or puffed-up stance of the enemies. My take on the words "proud" and "puffed" is inordinate pride. Another interpretation is presented by Theodore Hiebert drawing on the thought of J. J. M. Roberts. In a nutshell the fainthearted individual will not walk in the way of the vision.

> Look at the proud!
> Their spirit is not right in them,
> but the righteous live by their faith. (Hab 2:4)[16]

For Habakkuk faith connotes God's faithfulness or fidelity to vindicate the righteous Hebrews. Paul alludes to this verse in Romans 1:17, Paul wrote:

> For in it the righteousness of God is revealed through faith for faith; as it is written, "The one who is righteous will live by faith."

16. Hiebert, "Book of Habakkuk," 642.

Ever since Martin Luther the word "faith" has often been understood as belief. However, the New Testament Koine Greek word for faith can also be translated as "trust." Trust can be trust in Jesus, or the trust Jesus had in the fidelity of God, or God's trustworthiness. The trust Jesus had in God his heavenly Father converges with Habakkuk's faith in God's trustworthiness and faithfulness. As suggested in chapter 3 of Habakkuk, in time, God will save his people. The future is distant in this eschatological book. Whether Habakkuk wrote this poem of trust or if it was added, the thrust of trust in God's strength flows from Habakkuk's commission to write the vision. A later editor could have picked up on the flow. Have you ever been in a poetry-writing group when another poet knew where you were headed before you did? Such are my fanciful thoughts as a poet.

Paul asked his people to ponder poetically. In Philippians 1:9–11 Paul recorded his prayer in which he prays for his people to grow in discernment which is both a poetic and judicial task. "And it is my prayer that your love may abound more and more, with knowledge and all discernment, so that you may approve what is excellent, and may be pure and blameless for the day of Christ, filled with the fruits of righteousness which come through Jesus Christ, to the glory and praise of God" (RSV).

There is an inkling of poetic contemplation in his word "discernment" and judicial judgments in Paul's use of the word "approve." The New Testament Koine Greek word for "discernment" means "perception or apprehension by the senses." The Greek word for "discernment" (*aisthēsi*) means "perception or apprehension by the senses." The Greek work for "approve" (*dokimazein*) means "examine, to determine its purity." Paul throughout his ministry is an assayer examining morality. Poets apprehend, perceive, sense, and discern. Discerning like a poet and determining like a judge together suggest a prayerful thought process of poetic perception and just determining. Discerning poetically and determining justly are interrelated processes that build upon and enrich the other. In a nutshell, Paul prays that Christians will perceive poetically and judge judiciously.

Fulfillment of the double metaphor of poet-prophet and just judge is most fully present in 1 Corinthians. Prophecy—however poetic—and judgment—however just—do not have the last words. Love has the final say. Paul the poet preacher proclaims in 1 Corinthians 13 that love never ends, but prophecies will come to an end (13:8). Then the need for prophecy will end. Poetry will still be needed to praise and sing.

Both men and women made in the image of God can emulate the derivative metaphor of God as just judge and poet-prophet. Therefore this image is inclusive. I believe that the mixed metaphor of God as just judge and poet-prophet is what G. B. Caird called "commissive" in *The Language and Imagery of the Bible*. He wrote: "Many metaphors are commissive. If I call God 'Father' I commit myself to filial dependence and obedience." He went on to credit D. D. Evans with the name "outlook" to this type of metaphor. "I look on God as father, king, judge, shepherd, sculptor and commit myself to the attitudes or conduct which any of these implies."[17]

What then does it mean to look upon God anthropomorphically as just judge and poet-prophet? To my mind, this metaphor suggests a God whose roles transcend sex, is just and open to discussion through prayer about what justice means in the present and future. As a poet, God can deal with ambiguity, encourage questioning, and values well-chosen words. God speaks in dreams and vision to evoke our prayers and poetic play. With a prophet's voice God reminds us of our responsibility and the open future. With a poet's heart God values the work of writers. Perhaps the humanities are God's auxiliary.

I also must answer my own question. What does it mean to me to look to God as just judge and poet-prophet? To look to God as just judge is to promise to bring my mind and imagination to assess or judge what is fair. I must try hard to see all the angles and points of view. Questions about what is at stake for various people must be in my mind. Considering God's prophetic word is to remain open to justice and love, truth and beauty. Contemplating

---

17. Caird, *Language and Imagery of the Bible*, 153.

God as poet is realizing that God speaks to me through poetry and calls forth play with words.

While mindful that God is beyond all metaphors, imagining God as a just judge and poet-prophet is a charge that commissions women and men to go and be likewise by perceiving poetically and assessing justly.

For Further Thought

Is it possible for you to imaginatively enter into David's understanding of God without buying into his theology that equates disasters with punishment from God?

David's truths were formed by his cultural matrix of what is good in community. One example of the good in his community was monotheism, worshiping the true Rock. Therefore disasters which might serve to put people back on track could be perceived as goodness. Understandings of what is good evolve in communities and in the lives of individuals. Cultural matrixes change. Rising sea levels might put us on track to addressing climate change. Lifestyle might contribute to ill health. However, not every bad thing that can happen to people is their own fault or the result of sin. Sometimes people, even though faultless, have faulty genes or are in the wrong place at the wrong time. Without ignoring the original situation and ancient understandings of sin do praise of God, affirming meanings beyond ourselves, and the importance of having just rulers transcend the original time and place?

Because it is hard to imagine a completely just human ruler I have the following question: Is David's concept of a just ruler that reflects God's house as "is like the light of morning, like the sun rising on a cloudless morning, gleaming from the rain on the grassy land" an attempt to express something close to ineffable?

Bibliography

Alter, Robert. *The Art of Biblical Poetry.* New York: Penguin, 2011.

Alter Robert, and Frank Kermode. *The Literary Guide to the Bible.* Cambridge, MA: Belknap of Harvard University Press, 1987.

Bailey, James L., and Lyle D. Vander Broek. *Literary Forms in the New Testament: A Handbook.* Louisville: Westminster/John Knox, 1992.

Bainton, Roland H. *Here I Stand: A Life of Martin Luther.* Nashville: Abington, 1978.

Balentine, Samuel E. *Prayer in the Hebrew Bible: The Drama of Divine Human Dialogue.* Minneapolis, MN: Augsburg Fortress, 1993.

Berlin, Adele. "Introduction to Hebrew Poetry." In *The New Interpreter's Bible: General Articles & Introduction, Commentary, & Reflections for Each Book of the Bible, including the Apocryphal/Deuterocanonical Books,* edited by Leander K. Keck et al., 4:301–14. 12 vols. Nashville: Abingdon, 1994–2002.

Brown, Raymond E. *An Introduction to New Testament Christology.* New York: Doubleday, 1997.

Brueggemann, Walter. *Finally Comes the Poet: Daring Speech for Proclamation.* Minneapolis, MN: Augsburg Fortress, 1989.

Caird, George Bradford. *The Language and Imagery of the Bible.* Philadelphia, PA: Westminster, 1980.

Cameron, P. S. "Lead Us Not into Temptation." *Expository Times* 101.10 (1989) 299–301.

Carter, Warren, and Amy-Jill Levine. *The New Testament: Methods and Meanings.* Nashville: Abingdon, 2013.

Cooper, Alan. "Imagining Prophecy." In *Poetry and Prophecy: The Beginning of a Literary Tradition,* edited by James L. Kugel, 26–44. Ithaca: Cornell University Press, 1990.

Cullmann, Oscar. *Prayer in the New Testament: With Answers from the New Testament to Today's Questions.* Translated by John Bowden. London: SCM, 1995.

Durham, John I. *The Biblical Rembrandt: Human Painter in a Landscape of Faith.* Macon, GA: Mercer University Press, 2004.

Ferguson, Margaret W., et al., eds. *The Norton Anthology of Poetry.* 5th ed. New York: Norton, 2004.

Fisch, Harold. *Poetry with a Purpose: Biblical Poetics and Interpretation.* First Midland Book Edition. Bloomington: Indiana University Press, 1990.

Gabel, John B., and Charles B. Wheeler. *The Bible as Literature: An Introduction.* New York: Oxford University Press, 1990.

Greenberg, Moshe. *Biblical Prose Prayer.* London: University of California Press, 1983.

Harrington, Daniel J. "Lectio Divina: A Critical and Religious Reading of the Bible." *Huffington Post,* October 12, 2020. https://www.huffpost.com/entry/a-critical-and-religious-_b_1937193.

———. *Paul's Prisons Letters: Spiritual Commentaries on Paul's Letters to Philemon, the Philippians, and the Colossians.* New York: New City, 1997.

———. *Who Is Jesus? Why Is He Important? An Invitation to the New Testament.* Franklin, WI: Sheed & Ward, 1999.

Hiebert, Theodore. "The Book of Habakkuk." In *The New Interpreter's Bible: General Articles & Introduction, Commentary, & Reflections for Each Book of the Bible, including the Apocryphal/Deuterocanonical Books,* edited by Leander K. Keck et al., 7:623–55. 12 vols. Nashville: Abingdon, 1994–2002.

Homer. *The Odyssey: The Story of Odysseus.* Translated by W. H. D. Rouse. New York: Signet Classic by New American Library, 1999.

Hooker, Morna D. "The Letter to the Philippians." In *The New Interpreter's Bible: General Articles & Introduction, Commentary, & Reflections for Each Book of the Bible, including the Apocryphal/Deuterocanonical Books,* edited by Leander K. Keck et al., 11:468–549. 12 vols. Nashville: Abingdon, 1994–2002.

Hooper, Walter, ed. *Selected Literary Essays.* By C. S. Lewis. San Francisco: HarperOne, 2017.

Johnson, Luke Timothy. "Can We Still Believe in Miracles? We Can, We Must." *Commonweal,* February 12, 2019.

———. *The Gospel of Luke.* A Michael Glazier Book. Collegeville, MN: Liturgical, 1991.

Keck, Leander K., et al., eds. *The New Interpreter's Bible: General Articles & Introduction, Commentary, & Reflections for Each Book of the Bible, including the Apocryphal/Deuterocanonical Books.* 12 vols. Nashville: Abingdon, 1994–2002.

Kugel, James L. *The Great Poems of the Bible.* New York: Free Press, 1999.

Kugel, James L., ed. *Poetry and Prophecy: The Beginnings of a Literary Tradition.* Ithaca, NY: Cornell University Press, 1990.

Levine, Amy-Jill. *Selected Short Stories by Jesus: The Enigmatic Parables of a Controversial Rabbi.* San Francisco: HarperOne, 2014.

Levine, Amy-Jill, and Marc Zvi Brettler. *The Jewish Annotated New Testament.* New York: Oxford University Press, 2011.

Marchal, Joseph A. "Expecting a Hymn, Encountering An Argument: Introducing the Rhetoric of Philippians and Pauline Interpretation." *Journal of Biblical Theology* 6.3 (2007) 245–55.

McWhirter, Jocelyn. *Rejected Prophets: Jesus and His Witnesses in Lukes–Acts.* Minneapolis, MN: Augsburg Fortress, 2013.

Bibliography

Murray, Michele. "The First Letter of John." In *The Jewish Annotated New Testament*, edited by Amy-Jill Levine and Marc Zvi Brettler, 448–49. New York: Oxford University Press, 2011.

Perrin, Norman. *Jesus and the Language of the Kingdom: Symbol and Metaphor in New Testament Interpretation.* Philadelphia: Fortress, 1980.

Petersen, David L., and Kent Harold Richards. *Interpreting Hebrew Poetry.* Minneapolis: Augsburg Fortress, 1992.

Pick, John, trans. *A Hopkins Reader: Selections from the Writings of Gerard Manley Hopkins.* Image Books Edition. Garden City, NY: Doubleday, 1966.

Porter, Hugh, and Ethel K. Porter, eds. *Pilgrim Hymnal.* Boston: Pilgrim, 1958.

Richardson, Robert D., Jr. *Emerson: The Mind on Fire.* Berkley, CA: University of California Press, 1995.

Whallon, William. *Formula, Character, and Context: Studies in Homeric, Old English, and Old Testament Poetry.* Washington, DC: Center for Hellenic Studies, 1969.

Wilder, Amos N. *The Language of the Gospels: Early Christian Rhetoric.* New York: Harper & Row, 1964.

———. *Theopoetic: Theology and the Religious Imagination.* Minneapolis: Fortress, 1976.

www.ingramcontent.com/pod-product-compliance
Lightning Source LLC
Chambersburg PA
CBHW060425090426
42734CB00011B/2448